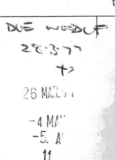

War Isn't Wonderful

Decorations by Douglas Hall

Other memoirs by Ursula Bloom

VICTORIAN VINAIGRETTE

THE ELEGANT EDWARDIAN

DOWN TO THE SEA IN SHIPS

YOUTH AT THE GATE

URSULA BLOOM

War isn't
Wonderful

HUTCHINSON OF LONDON

HUTCHINSON & CO. (Publishers) LTD
178–202 Great Portland Street, London, W.1

London Melbourne Sydney
Auckland Bombay Toronto
Johannesburg New York

★

First published 1961

This book has been set in Bembo type face. It has
been printed in Great Britain by The Anchor Press,
Ltd., in Tiptree, Essex, on Smooth Wove paper
and bound by Taylor Garnett Evans & Co., Ltd., in
Watford, Herts

Author's Note

THIS book claims to have no new aspect on war as a whole and is merely the everyday story of a woman's life during the years of uncertainty. She was too ill to serve in any capacity, restless by her own inaction, and emotionally deeply disturbed as to what the outcome would be.

To bring the reader level with the previous book of this series, *Youth at the Gate*, which ended on November 11th, 1918, may I give the facts of those conditions in which World War II found me?

In November 1925 I had remarried, Commander Gower Robinson, R.N. (Robbie). Early in the thirties he had retired from the Royal Navy because I had been stricken with paralysing headaches which had made me almost an invalid. These headaches were wrongly diagnosed and treated as being a form of migraine, but in the early fifties they were discovered to be caused by an arterial trouble and were cured by surgical operation.

Robbie was working in the Communications Department of H.M. Foreign Office, where he was very happy, and his life lay with cyphers. After years of living in hotels we had taken a Chelsea flat. Philip (Pip), the only child of my previous marriage, had married before the war began, in fact it caught him on honeymoon in the South of France.

I was a fairly successful novelist. I wrote plays for broadcasting, was beauty editor of *Woman's Own*, and was a reliable journalist.

It was in this state that World War II caught me and mine.

U.B.

Foreword

The entries are taken from the actual diaries I kept at the time and the dates may seem inaccurate because they were noted in accordance with the announcements given out, often two or three days late.

The Beginning

BECAUSE for me the Second World War began with the Munich crisis, before I start the book I must give some details of what happened then, and the immense effect that dreadful month of September had upon me emotionally. After that everybody save myself seemed to come through happily resolved that we had been very fortunate, and that now we really should have 'peace in our time'. The swords would be turned into ploughshares, said the optimistic.

I never felt the same way about it. I was, of course, condemned for my pessimism and my alarm as to our future, but none of us can help a personal doubt, and mine had been provoked when I had visited Germany in 1933.

9

I was sent out there by a newspaper to review the Passion Play at Oberammergau. I crossed to Ostend, and had a sleeper in the most chattering clattering train in which I have ever been supposed to sleep, from Ostend to Munich. When the dawn came and we had been noisily jolted into a siding I who could not sleep got up and looked out of the window. We were alongside a small town, and obviously they were preparing themselves for a large military review.

Until this moment I had allowed myself to be stupidly misled on the talk of German disarmament and thought the rumours had been greatly exaggerated by the Press. There had been articles in the papers stating that the Hun tanks being made of three-ply wood were utterly valueless martially; their main destiny was to impress the credulous public. Looking out of the window of my fetid sleeper I saw before me an enormous sea of tanks that certainly were not made of three-ply wood, and appeared to me to be clankingly real. Let me admit the truth—they terrified me, and at that moment I saw the grim shadow of things to come.

On my return to England I reported this incident to someone who I thought should know, and was told, 'Of course they make them *look* real, but they aren't really so,' which left me hopelessly unconvinced. We had gone ahead blind to our danger. We were all ostriches sticking our heads in the sand, and as far as I could see the sand was getting burningly hot.

The Munich crisis crept up behind us, quietly; suddenly I woke to the fact that something was wrong.

'What's happening?' I asked Robbie, as we sat in the peach-and-lime lounge of our very attractive flat. It was the period when a daily maid 'did' for us. We had little intimacy with the washing-up, and less with the household cleaning. At the time Robbie was wanting his tea, then an importance to the hard-worked male, though today in the sixties it has become rather 'Mrs. Gaskell'.

'Oh, just Hitler!' he said. 'One of these days the balloon will go up, but I don't think it will be now.'

'Anything funny in the cyphers?'

He gave me that horny look of the naval officer when he thinks his honour is insulted. 'If there were I shouldn't tell you,' he replied.

Men are made that way. They have not the share-and-share-alike amiability of most women. I asked, 'If there *is* a war,' (awful thought!), 'I wonder how we think we could win it?'

He said, again with the cool glory of the Senior Service, 'The Navy is here for that.'

I have always felt that it must be quite marvellous to be so sure of anything. I am never doggedly certain; deep within me there is always that recurring doubt which asks, '*But why?*' However, one does not argue with a gentleman who is so impressive. One rings the bell for tea and buttered buns. Later in the day I rang up Wyatt Tilby, a famous political correspondent, the man who urged me to start in Fleet Street, and whom I could trust.

'What's happening?' I asked.

He told me, and he told me without frills on it. It was apparently one of those European crises to which we now seemed to be annually committed, and, although he believed that this one would blow over—obviously we should eat humble pie, it seemed to be our main dish these days—sooner or later there would undoubtedly be war.

'But not yet?' I asked. It is a crazy human fact that when faced with the horror of modern warfare one always prays, '*Not yet!*' I suppose the terror of our outraged imagination demands this of us.

'Probably next year.'

I said, 'Oh!'

That was the Munich crisis.

The First World War had struck me hard when I was in the teens, and when it broke had inspired me with the glorious stimulation of a frenzied patriotism. But during the years of hostilities I had learnt that 'patriotism is not enough', as Edith

Cavell said; I had learnt the humiliation and the agony of it all. In 1914 I was playing the piano in a Harpenden cinema, and the very strains of 'Land of Hope and Glory' could thrill me with exultation. In 1918 I never batted an eyelid when I heard it, for my patriotism, in company with the deeply stirred emotion of thousands of other young people, had died in France, where the earth had turned red with the blood of our poor young men among the poppies.

In that first world war a great deal had happened to me that was agonizing, terrifying, and vile. It would, I knew, be worse this time.

Two days later in that tragic September of 1938 we were driving down to spend the afternoon at Lamorbey Park, which is just outside Sidcup, at that time a charming village. Lamorbey Park was a mansion which had once belonged to the Malcolms, Lily Langtry's family, standing in delightful grounds and run as a pleasant country hotel by Mr. Sheppard (commonly known as Bertie) and his wife. We had spent so many happy summers there and often went down. Going across Blackheath we saw something a little unusual, and coming to Kidbrooke R.A.F. Depot we saw what appeared to be a captive balloon quivering over the sprawling field. Were we now going ballooning again, or what? Little did I know, as we guessed as to what it could be, that the hour would come when we thanked heaven for those clumsily bulging balloons, for they would represent some shallow sort of security to stem the fury of enemy attack.

I have always kept a diary, and here are the entries that I made in those days.

September 7th, 1938

The war news having been better all day, is tonight quite dreadful again, and the prospect of what this could mean, terrifying. I do not want another generation of young people to suffer as we did before. Yet what can we do?

September 9th, 1938

This has been the worst day of suspense, and the tension is quite horrible (I cannot eat). We have not yet told Hitler that we shall have to support the Czechs, but surely we must?

September 11th, 1938

War seems to be very near indeed, and if it comes too many will die, and too many have their whole lives blighted, and the whole of civilization will be changed. Has the world no sense? and what can a single person like myself do to put a spanner in the works?

September 12th, 1938

Today matters appear to be worsening, and there seems to be little doubt that it must come. I ought to be doing something, but what can one actually *do*? This is where the Horsemen of the Apocalypse always get one beat! It is a lovely warm day, to me the more tragic because it is England at its best, and most of the people seem to be courageously unconcerned, and far more occupied with their holidays. It was like that last time. Perhaps they do not realize the horror of what could be coming.

September 14th, 1938

The Prime Minister is to go to see Hitler tomorrow. This is a marvellous effort for an old man to make, something that has never been done before, and even if it all goes wrong we should be proud of him. At least he is doing something to stem the tide, and I personally should have thought the bravery of the individual effort was the only chance to save the situation.

Next morning, when the *Daily Express* was pushed through the letter-box, there was this announcement in it:

'. . . Then, in his quiet voice, and leaning back in his big armchair at the Cabinet table, a thumb in his waistcoat armhole, Mr. Chamberlain made the sudden suggestion that he should go over to see Hitler.

'There was silence at the table when he finished his short statement. Ministers could not at first take in the boldness of the stroke. The Prime Minister, one eyebrow raised inquiringly, a thin smile on his lips, looked round the table.

'One after another the Ministers expressed their agreement, their admiration for Mr. Chamberlain's courage. I am told that Mr. Chamberlain listened to the short discussion in silence, then he said, "Well, I take it that is agreed?" At once he wrote out a telegram for despatch to Hitler through the British Embassy in Berlin:

'*In view of the increasingly critical situation, I propose to come over at once to see you, with a view of trying to find a peaceful solution. I propose to come across by air, and am ready to start tomorrow. Please indicate earliest time at which you can see me, and suggest a place of meeting. Should be grateful for a very early reply.*

NEVILLE CHAMBERLAIN'

Even in the light of subsequent events and harsh criticisms one can only say that this was the action of a very brave man and admire the courage that inspired it. Neville Chamberlain knew even at that time that he had an inoperable cancer; he must have felt desperately ill, tiring too easily, yet he flung himself nobly into the abyss, believing that his personal effort was the only hope of saving the situation. What I do not think he anticipated was the horror of that interview with a screaming maniac.

My next entry shows the disappointment he must have felt.

September 16th, 1938

Hope fell again when we learnt that Mr. Chamberlain was returning at once, but rose tonight for he states that he will be back to see Herr Hitler in Cologne. He must have had a shocking interview, poor fellow.

The suspense was becoming very alarming, for the crisis had sprung upon us so unexpectedly out of the blue and was all the worse for that. Young men had started to dig trenches on Wandsworth Common—we could see them working by flares in the late evening when we went over to Balham to see my father. They were vigorous young men, and women, who like myself so much wanted to do *something*, and this was what they thought might help.

My father was at this time seventy-nine, remarried, to Jo—amiable but brainless—and they were living in unfurnished rooms in Ryde Vale Road. Although my father was so old he still had the infinite capacity for work which runs in the Blooms. He had retired from the Church when he remarried, was a famous genealogist and archivist, and a skilled author. A big stout man, his red hair was now thistledown soft and white, the curls gone, but his face was florid, and the blue eyes merry.

Neither of us knew even where my brother was; he had a capacity for wandering off into the blue, had married, and had then cut himself off from his family.

'We can get along quite well without him,' said my father cheerfully, for he never let that sort of thing worry him. It worried me, for I am a sentimentalist and adore family life. He did not care. I told him how I felt about the war.

'It hasn't come yet,' he said, 'and maybe it won't.'

'It will one day, everybody says that.'

'Yes, perhaps that is true,' he agreed, 'but if it doesn't come today that at least is something.'

I suppose he was a fatalist, and his assurance of it not being today was all part of my own first response when Mr. Tilby had said war must come and I had answered, 'Not yet?'

Humanity is made this way.

Jo did not seem anxious. She was rather an inane old lady,

confident that whatever happened it would be all right, and not bothering herself about it, which in a way was a good thing. War is always so much worse for the old.

September 22nd, 1938

Chamberlain has failed, and now the war is actually on our threshold. We learnt this tonight, after a grim day when hope gradually died. Last time when I knew it was coming I found it quite inspiring, 'Long Way to Tipperary' stuff, today it horrifies me. Perhaps I am getting very old. . . .

September 24th, 1938

My headache is appalling, and I am getting so sick of all this war worry. First we are going to fight, then we aren't. Would it not be almost better if we behaved like stern Papa, and said, 'Now come on, or get out, and if you *do* come on, you're for it!' Up with the fist. The Czechs have had to give in. I cannot bear to think what they must be suffering, for if our plight is bad, theirs is far worse.

September 26th, 1938

Will our wait-and-see government ever pull up its socks? Or have they no socks? Hyde Park is now being dug for trenches. I wish I could dig. Gas masks are to be served out and the ones that I have seen look to be quite awful. I suppose they are not meant to be becoming?

September 27th, 1938

Went to see my father and whilst I was sitting talking to him in his pleasant room, the cars were going down the street with loud speakers giving instructions where to get your gas-mask. He is so awfully brave, just doesn't give a damn. Still says it hasn't come yet, and if it does he'll join the A.R.P. and do war work. He probably will, too.

I got a gas-mask from Chelsea town hall, and then they sent a fat girl round to fetch it back, because apparently I had got the one they called Willie, and it leaks! Another foreboding of things to come. We aren't really very clever, are we?

Tonight the main tubes are closed so that they can be converted into shelters. Chamberlain spoke on the radio and sounded dreadfully tired.

September 28th, 1938

We went down into Sussex and I saw Pip [my son]. He wanted my advice about which service to join when it comes, but I think the selection of pistols or swords is a man's individual right. It seems wrong to give advice. Once I was proud that we had an armistice which was the end of wars. Now this. And it won't only happen again now, but again ahead, for war seems to be part of man's inheritance.

I had refused to consent to Pip marrying Pamela until now, but with war overshadowing us, and perhaps so little time for any of us, I could only give it freely. The marriage if it comes can only fail, but that is his life. None of us live for ever; we all make mistakes.

The Fleet is called up.

Later

This tension is really too much for now another bombshell has dropped and Mr. Chamberlain is to meet Mussolini in Munich tomorrow. It's so awful, the rising and falling hopes. It's like running a fever temperature and then getting the ague.

B

September 29th, 1938

I have felt exhausted with anguish today. God, how I do hate war and whatever we do this won't help any one of us. Win or lose, it is always checkmate. The trenches look to be very deep. The air station in Kensington Gardens is loading up with ammunition, and I should have thought one German bomb on that should be a treat for the Serpentine Lido! Mr. Chamberlain is in Munich.

September 30th, 1938

I was in Weldon's office in Southampton Street this afternoon talking future work with Julia Cairns, when she got the news that after all it was going to be peace. Chamberlain had done it. There was an enormous crowd round the Palace tonight waiting for the P.M.'s return, and the Westminster and St. Margaret's chimes were going hot and strong. We went in the car. Presently the dead-tired P.M. came along in his car, going to the Palace amidst the loudest cheers that I have ever heard. He looked like some elderly raven, grey with fatigue, and years older. Later he came on to the balcony with the King and Queen. The King looked so happy about it. I shall never forget the noise of the cheering.
Chamberlain promised 'Peace in our time'.

October 1st, 1938

This is a real old blind, for London has gone mad, and most of them seem to be being sick in the gutters, whilst others sing 'Land of Hope and Glory' again!

Yet by the end of the year the impetuosity of that sudden joy had thawed a trifle, for, although the promise of peace in our time had been believed, now the first sign of fraying threads was making itself felt. My diary for the year ended like this:

December 31st, 1938

The snow is clearing off, but it has been very heavy indeed, and there are drifts everywhere. I am in bed with the most shocking cold. Pip is in Switzerland, Davos, with the future in-laws and now has wired to me that the engagement has been broken off, and would we meet him at Croydon aerodrome at 1.a.m. when he is due there! He really is the most trying young son to have. 'That'll be nice for your cold,' said Robbie with full naval epithets to boot. 'Let him damn' well get back himself!'
We all believe that we are at peace. It is the night of Ring out the Old, Ring in the New, and God only knows what the new can have in store for us. I am bewilderingly unhappy about it, for I still think that we should have fought Hitler last summer. I am becoming more sure of this.

One thing is clear, between the last day of September and the last one of the following December something had convinced me that we had done the wrong thing.

I believe I came to that decision when I went down to Swindon to open a fête there for Father Ronald Royle at St. Mark's vicarage. He and I walked out together into the lovely flowery garden on a hot autumn day which was truly lovely.

I said: 'Thank goodness we aren't at war. We could have been.'

I remember Father's cassock pirouetting up the dust of the gravel path which twined in between michaelmas daisies and button chrysanths. He had a bare head, and his very bright eyes shone as he turned to me. He said: 'We did the wrong thing. We should have kept our word, for we let the Czechs down. I always feel that it can never pay to break your word.'

A moment later I was on the platform making my introductory speech, but what he had said stayed fast with me, and I have thought of it many times since then. We *did* let the Czechs down to save ourselves and we have *not* saved ourselves.

It can never pay to break your word.

The Second World War

I

This war, like the next war, is a war to end wars.
OLD PROVERB

ON SEPTEMBER 3rd, 1939, Robbie added this entry to his personal diary:

'During the night I put into cypher the message which declared war on Germany if she did not accede to our terms, which of course she didn't, and we are now at war.'

21

He had despatched the message at 3 a.m. on the morning of the day on which our modern world was to change.

*   *   *

I was staying at Moreton-in-Marsh at the time because I had been very far from well. The headaches were appalling. This time when the crisis came England received it with an amazingly cold scorn. Last year we had rushed about trying to escape; this year we had garrisoned our homes, deciding to spend the period of hostilities *in* our homes, and to prepare for the worst.

There must be no more of this 'peace in our time'. We'd had that one. Peace was on the way out and we would fight and be damned to it.

But with my headaches so bad that at times I was in a coma with them, Robbie wanted to get me away, and I had come near to the rectory where I was brought up. Moreton had a moderate train service, and Robbie could come down every other night. So we had slipped out of London for the time being and had come down here.

Even before the war came the face of England was changing rapidly, and in those last few days of our paltry peace the fingerprints of war itself were already on us.

I was trying to learn again to drive a car. Although I had driven—in a way—since 1922, that had been at a time when my brother had told me car driving was 'just like riding a bicycle', with the result that that I trusted to the brake and never used the gears. I just shot into top, went like a bird, and had some most disastrous results.

Seeing war ahead Robbie had tried to teach me a different method in Battersea Park. Left alone with the car at Moreton, I knew just sufficient to get her on to the road (little more), and I tried to teach myself. After all, fools did drive cars, why not me?

I had my awkward moments what with the local hens and dogs, the traffic lights on the Cirencester road, and cows ambling along to the milking sheds, all of which sent me into a complete tizzy.

I took the car back to my home village, quite forgetting that the place being situated in a blind alley of a lane I should be pushed into the embarrassing position of having to turn round, and had a very worrying afternoon there.

I was confronted with an almost super-human problem by the paddock gate, which made me forget the coming war. It took me a full twenty minutes, and during that time I had marked the ditch for ever, knocked down a small sapling, and had banged the paddock gate with gusto, leaving peculiar abrasions on the car which I only hoped Robbie would never notice.

But I did it, and returned to Moreton in some triumph at having achieved what I considered to be a major victory.

The village was perturbed by the coming war. They are a kind people—a people I have known all my life—and I was furious that there was so little one could do to help them. The young men who were on the Reserve were actually called up out of the harvest fields. They came with their sickles in their hands.

Then the evacuee children from the cities started to arrive in their squads. They were pitifully brave, clasping their gas-masks and their labels.

In our little post office Annie was the postmistress. I had known Annie all my life, a giggler, a joyful amiable friendly person who always thought life 'ever so foony'. In her sixties, she was a simple woman and she was now saddled with four evacuee girls, which she found a problem.

'It's their hair,' she said—Annie was always almost absurdly clean—and then in a solemn voice, 'It's them things!'

'Not nits?'

She could not say the dreadful word. 'It's awful,' she said, 'just awful.'

This nit problem was not confined to the post office, every-body was finding it in their nice clean cottages, and worse. Also the children had not the same rules as regards their manners.

Some were not even house-trained like the lowest mongrel pup in the village. Many of the little back-streets-of-Birmingham toughs had never sat down to a set meal and could not think why they had to do it now. But they fell for the good, sound, country food. Annie took their lunch out to a table under the garden elm. Sunday was roast lamb with onion sauce. She stopped them from eating the lamb with their fingers, and gasped when they ate the onion sauce with the ginger pudding.

'They're ever so foony,' said Annie.

But of course the children had their own angle. What did nits matter? Everybody had them. Why couldn't they buy fish-and-chips? Where was the cinema? Oh hell! They asked why we hadn't got a copper. Shown the one in the kitchen with some pride by Annie, who did nothing if not take life stolidly literally, they said a real copper was what they meant. In Whitchurch we had never kept that sort of copper. There was one at Alderminster, which was conveniently situated three miles away, and as far as the village was concerned Alderminster was welcome to him and could keep him, whilst we gaily poached through the night. As his beat covered about eight miles of fairly wild country, the chances were that our poaching would continue undisturbed, and we all felt so it ought.

One earnest little boy started a betting establishment at one cottage; others stole what they could, and kicked their landladies' shins. One beat up the pigs with sticks. 'And the poor things covered with the most awful wales,' said Annie; then with tears: 'They're not like us. Do you know my little girls have never been to church?' and in horror, 'They asked me what it was!'

It didn't surprise me. It surprised me even less that Annie never got them to church, but, be it said to her credit, she *did* get rid of the nits, and she *did* insist on grace before meat.

I visited Elsie, once our cook and married to our very nice gardener Ernest. She was apprehensive and nervous of bombing coming there. I tried to persuade her that I did not think Hitler would want to bomb the village—it was too small and much too countrified. I only hope that she believed me and took fresh heart.

I then went to Preston-on-Stour, the next village to ours (something of a foreign country, of course), as I had always cared for old Mrs. Horseman at the post office there. Some fool had told the poor old lady that the moment the Germans landed the church bells would be rung to warn everyone to beware. Naturally she had a fit! She said she would die if she heard the church bells ringing, she just could not bear it. I put my arms round her and tried to convince her that nothing is as bad as you expect it to be, and whilst this was going on the bells started their weekly practice and that nearly killed her.

As I drove back to Moreton along the Ilmington road, I felt that I would never forgive Germany's dictator for upsetting so many nice people so much. And under all this lay my personal fear, unpatriotic I admit, as to whether we should win this war or not. Wyatt Tilby had told me that he considered that victory or defeat depended entirely on whether Hitler tried to run the show himself or left it to his generals. Privately I thought that Hitler would never be such a fool as to try it.

*   *   *

War coming rapidly nearer, England prepared for the blackout. Instructions were given us in almost a merry voice over the radio, and there ensued a ghastly week-end when one could not buy another quarter of a yard of blackout material anywhere. That was followed by the somewhat desperate effort of trying to nail the curtains to windows framed in Cotswold stone, which was extremely painful. One couldn't buy another tintack in Moreton-in-Marsh, try as one would. One rushed from town to town in the search, and life was bewilderingly exhausting.

I had a letter from my father at Balham. He had been thinking things over and had come to the conclusion that he must take up war service of some sort. He disregarded the fact that this year he would be eighty, and to my horror had trotted along to the Auxiliary Fire Service headquarters and some fool had let him sign on. He had filled in the form, giving his age as being 'over sixty', which was true, of course, but misleading. He was gaily young-looking, and had that charm and persuasive manner of our family which jockeyed him over most hurdles, and got him what he wanted, but it didn't last. At his first practice he had to crawl through barrels, and the old tum could not do it. He was furious.

I had now come to the point when I just wanted to get the wretched war started, seeing that there was no other way out. There was no declaration on the Saturday, as we had expected, and I was still rushing round Warwickshire in the car trying desperately to get more blackout material, with no sign of any. The nine o'clock news that night told us nothing, and Robbie was on duty till the next morning at the Foreign Office. I did not know of course that at 3 a.m. he would despatch *the* fatal telegram.

Sunday was radiantly lovely.

It seems that all the marked days in the history of England have this loveliness. The place was peaceful. I looked down into the garden of the hotel with its hedges of lavender daisies and the big double sunflowers everywhere which looked so like the Victorian brooches that my great-aunts wore. The mulberry trees smelt of a honeyed warmth, and in the orchard at the far end there was the carmine glow of Worcester pearmains amongst the mature green. I thought what a beautiful thing it can be when autumn comes to a fruiting garden, even though it whispers of the year's ending! This might be the end of an epoch, too. It could be the end of so many happy lives—and for nothing.

I wondered (as most silly women wondered) what real difference this war would make to me. How much would my country change? Although it changed in 1914–18, when the roaring twenties came it had gone back to a similar pattern as before, in a modified way. Now the people about me were saying it would all be over by Christmas (they said that last time). What would I do if the R.N. recalled Robbie? How could I cope with these terrific headaches which at times sent me into comas? The Femergin injections? The awful aftermath of pain? What would happen to my son? He had married this autumn and had slipped out of our lives in the way modern young people often do.

I thought of this past summer when, realizing war was at our heels, Robbie and I had gone to Cumberland to 'say goodbye to the dear lakes there'. We had stood looking at Wastwater, with the black scree slipping down into it and turning the whole lake dark, and we had promised each other that when it was all over we would come back and be happy again there.

When it was over!

I tried to write but was restless, ill at ease, perhaps desperately unhappy would be a better way of expressing it. The church bells were ringing and I turned on the portable wireless I had with me. That was when I heard Neville Chamberlain speaking of 'evil things' and giving us the fact that we were at war. His voice faded out. The bells had finished now but the birds still sang on in the garden, and a maidservant (it was the era of maidservants) was picking apples in the orchard and she came across a dewy lawn, holding up an apron full of them.

If this was the beginning of a greater England, of stronger faith, and of men and women being welded closer together in patriotism and loyalty, then it was the start of a happier era, but would that happen?

I went up to the funny little station to meet the 12.30 train, and when Robbie got out of the carriage he looked very tired, almost grey with it, and worn out.

'Did Chamberlain say we were at war?' he asked, for he had been in the train at eleven o'clock.

'Yes, he did.'

'So that's that.'

'Yes, I suppose it is.' People make stupid remarks when they are emotionally distraught. We walked out of the quiet station yard, with its smell of late roses and its vigorous profusion of asters in dark cerise and violent purple. After a time I said, 'What do you think will happen next?'

'Your guess is as good as mine. How could anybody know?'

Then we walked to the hotel in silence.

Robbie slept through the early part of the afternoon—a warm beautiful one—and they were playing croquet downstairs. I could hear the sharp impact of mallet and ball and it awakened memories of my girlhood when we had spent many hours that way. When Robbie woke we had tea on the lawn, with England rural and quite beautiful, as it often is on a Sunday afternoon in summer. Nothing had changed. The quiet seemed to be almost all wrong. I remember we had ratafia biscuits and home-made seed cake, and that there were little meths lamps under the tea-kettles, again reminiscent of my childhood.

'Let's go out somewhere in the car,' Robbie said that evening.

We went to Lower Slaughter, which I always think is the most lovely of the Cotswold villages. The thatched cottages clustered together, with roses pressing fat faces against the lath-and-plaster; the gardens were smudges of colour blurred together in a rich galaxy of warmth. We sat for a time in the car, watching the peacefulness of the water and smelling the nutty scents of earliest autumn, till after a while a smoky mist arose. When we drove home we hardly talked. There were the white lines completed along the road centres, new to us but making driving much easier, and all the villages were darkened.

I said, 'If it is as dark as this surely it is going to be very dangerous for everybody, even if a bomb never drops?'

'They'll drop all right,' he said glumly. Robbie is an arch pessimist in some ways, yet his clouds have had far more silver linings than mine, and always I am convinced that some day, somehow, the most superb silver lining will pop up for me and be there for ever.

Next morning came the news of the sinking of the *Athenia*.

'This is where we came in,' I said to Robbie, 'it's happened before. It's all so absurd, it shouldn't *be*, for nobody ever wins a war really.'

'I know,' he said.

*   *   *

The first air-raid warning came at Moreton when Robbie was in London. It was at 7.35 on the morning of the sixth. I happened to be in bed reading, and instantly shot up and grabbed the gas-mask. I dashed into my clothes, had a last furtive look through the mullioned window beyond which absolutely nothing was happening, then went downstairs as arranged.

The residents had collected in the lounge, the idea being with the reminder of the 1914–18 hostilities that if one stood with one's back to the main wall of the house nothing could possibly happen to the person—I suppose it is very satisfactory to be so sure. Nothing happened to any of us.

One gets a little tired of standing with one's back to the main wall *ad infinitum*, so I sat down and did some of my knitting. The milkman, making the most of an exciting occasion, came round and said that Romford had been raided, and that Chatham was already in ruins! All sorts of things were going on on the east coast, and I, who had lived there in the previous war, thought this quite likely. An hour later, when the all-clear was sounded, I felt silly as I took my gas-mask back upstairs and then started a belated breakfast away from the main wall of the house.

When Robbie came down he said there had been a warning in London but never so much as the buzz of enemy aircraft. He thought someone had done it for a joke, and if we were going to have tomfool jokes like this it was a pretty poor sort of a war.

In the early afternoon I went over to Preston, because I thought I ought to see how poor old Mrs. Horseman had taken it, as she had been so worried. I'd forgotten that she was deaf so hadn't heard the warning at all, and had spent the morning getting on with her washing in blissful ignorance of it all. In the village Ernest was what they called 'our R.A.P. Warden'. He had arisen of course and had got out his bicycle, but at that stage his first job was to go over to Alderminster to the pub there, get orders (possibly his whistle as well), and then come back before he got going. Alderminster is about three miles by bicycle!

'You know, all this is surely a bit amateur?' I said to Robbie.

'A bit? A damned big bit if you ask me!'

Gradually war filtered into our midst, and the Terriers were in camp in the fields and the local girls enjoying every moment of it. Whilst we ate our breakfasts at the hotel, soldiers did their P.T. on the grass verge of the main street, and I felt sorry for them for as the year went on and the real chilliness began their noses were so pink.

At home Robbie had sent most of the furniture into store in Croydon, keeping one bedroom and a bleak sitting-room at the flat, on the principle that war was no time to have all your eggs in one basket.

We were settling down to it slowly.

On the following Saturday we learnt that petrol was to be rationed, and down to six gallons a month, which terrified me. Like most evacuees I was miserably unhappy at Moreton; in-action has never been the main dish in the menu of my life and I loathed it. The declaration of war had done nothing to change any of this, though the P.M. had stated on the radio that we were 'progressing favourably', as though England were some invalid lady suffering from a nervous disease.

As we came nearer to the last week of unrationed petrol, Robbie instructed me to beg, borrow, or steal whatever I could get and store it in the garage, as other people were doing. This kept me busy. My great-great-grandmother having been of gypsy origin, these instructions suited me fine, and I even forgot that we were at war in the slick way in which I settled down to the job in hand.

Moreton early ran out of petrol. Stratford seemed to be frightfully smug over it. I picked up a couple of gallons at Clifford Chambers and another little lot on the Old Fosse Way, from a chatty young gentleman who sold it saying that only one person could get it, couldn't he? So it might just as well be me. (It *was* me!) And then he told me that he didn't think the war would come to much, you could see it wasn't working out, couldn't you? Which had some element of truth in it.

I was not happy at teatime on Saturday, because I did not feel that my resources were adequate, and I had just settled down to tea and buttered buns when someone said there was a garage along the Oxford road which still had plenty. To hell with buttered buns! said I and out I went. However, when I rounded the last corner of the Oxford road to the garage it was only too obvious that everyone else in Warwickshire, Worcestershire, and Gloucestershire had heard of this glorious truth. The queue was monumental. I felt that the petrol was bound to run out before I ever drew level with the pumps, but I got there and they still had some. What was more they had two of those enchanting big cans into which I could pop the lot and take it home. These had been off the market since Wednesday last, so it was almost too good to be true. 'Victory!' I told myself in triumph, 'I've won the war!' as I turned for home, wondering if one of the tin drums at the back got a spark on it would I blow up? And what then?

I shoved the car in the garage and rushed up to the station to meet Robbie. 'You don't know what I've got!' I said.

Men are not demonstrative.

They never share that noble high floodtide of female enthusiasm.

Having instructed me to get the stuff, now he eyed me with naval admonition in his eye. 'I wonder if it's patriotic,' he said.

The next week at Moreton got me really low. There was nothing to do but write or read, and I daren't use the car. Even my diary became rather tabloid.

September 15th, 1939

Took some photographs for something to do. Took two cows, and another of five beige ducks on a filthy pond.

September 16th, 1939

Nothing happens. Fine weather. Lots of wasps. Dahlias look lovely, asters nearly dead. Gladioli grand. My head awful.

September 17th, 1939

I do pray we win this rotten war, but it looks bad to me.

Then, on the Monday:

I am going to London tomorrow, Robbie says I may. I feel like Moses getting to the promised land, but wonder if the milk and honey is really there.

*   *   *

London had changed unbelievably, I could never have thought that it would have altered so much. As my train neared the terminus I saw for the first time the myriads of great balloons in the sky quivering above a city that had become almost alien to me. In the streets wherever one looked there were not only the soldiers, the sailors, and airmen, but the most formidable-looking women in uniform. Piccadilly Tube was closed, and there were sandbags everywhere. At the end of the day, when I came back to Moreton with Robbie, I was glad to return for the new London was so confusing.

'Stay here one wee bit longer,' he told me.

So for a while I was an evacuee, living through those first dormant weeks of war that was no war. I fretted dismally. I was alone and disheartened with no signs of the great push being made. Nothing happened.

September 25th, 1939

I am most miserably unhappy here, and cannot bear another day of it. I sit and cry and ought to be ashamed of it all, for Robbie is so good in coming down every other night. But the snag is, how *do* we plan a future?

September 26th, 1939

A ghastly headache with almost unendurable pain. I wonder how one lives, and dare not think of days ahead with it. When Robbie came down tonight I think he realized how miserable I was.

September 27th, 1939

A wonderful harvest moon, and one of those too glorious days of yellow leaves against a blue sky. Robbie says that if the raids come and are not too awful, I can go home. Miracle! Here I am utterly lost without the car.

By October 1st I was in bed with one of the worst colds of my life and it was plain that something would have to be done about my wretched body. I could not even write, and when that happens it is death to me. By the end of the month I had moved to Banbury where at least I could go to the cinema if I wanted to. There was one at Moreton, but the only time I went I had to nurse a large lumpy child for its mother, because it felt sick. I didn't go again. On November 4th there is one magic entry in my diary, no comment, only the straight fact: 'I am going *home*!'

Perhaps this is the worst of being born nostalgic, for on holidays it becomes a positive disease with me, and I suffer deeply

C

through it. All I wanted was to get back, to dig myself in, and be permanently with Robbie. So we returned. On Pip's birthday I wrote glowingly: 'I am home. Evacuation was too awful.'

I finally came to the conclusion that this cold war was the cleverest thing that Herr Hitler had ever done, for it left us completely baffled. Were we at war or were we not? Nobody had got the right answer to this.

I had been back for three whole days to the depleted flat (for everything possible was in store) when I made a bid for the future. Without Robbie knowing, I arranged for the furniture to be brought back. The van with it arrived early and waited round the corner of the street until the man in charge had seen Robbie depart for the Foreign Office, then bounced round to the door and started on the good work. It was a breathless day for all of us, and just before five in the evening, when Robbie was due back, we finished it. I hid in the bathroom as the sound of his key in the lock was heard. The door opened, he stepped across the threshold, paused, then boomed, 'Good God!'

He had come into the home which was exactly as he had known it when war first came. We were back again.

2

'Tis all a chequer board of nights and days,
Where destiny with men for pieces plays.
OMAR KHAYYÁM

WE WERE now well advanced into the first phase of the war. My headaches were tragically bad. We were a restless and unsettled people, realizing that we lived on the brink of a volcano and at any moment it might erupt. Christmas came and went in a thick fog, whilst the new year was celebrated with the first of the peace parties (or so we thought them then), and I finished 1939 with this effective note in my diary:

Goodbye, old year, 1939 was dud!

* * *

With the new spring I started doing a little war work but the headaches made me unreliable, so that I was ashamed. I went to Selfridge's to receive H.H. Princess Marie Louise, who was to accept purses and knitted contributions there for the *Daily Sketch* War Relief Fund. I waited at the far end of the room for her to come to me, curtseyed deeply, and she was so utterly charming. 'The horror is that I myself knit so badly,' she murmured, as we sat down to receive the contributions.

My eye went down the approaching queue of contributors and about halfway I saw a schoolboy. He would have been about ten years old, with four pairs of obviously home-made socks under his arm and a brightly scarlet face. He got redder as he came nearer, but was determined. I could not warn the Princess that there was something odd afoot because she was so busy receiving, and this wretched child took his turn at speed, banged down those beastly socks with one hand and with the other proffered a sweet-sticky autograph book, saying, 'Your auto-graph, please, miss?'

For a moment the Princess was completely taken aback, then she demurred, and with praiseworthy agility passed him on to the lady-in-waiting by her side.

For the same fund I went with Lady Oxford, Mabel Con-standuros, and Dennis Wheatley (though what he was doing there I simply cannot imagine) to Arding and Hobbs'. I made my speech knitting all the time and actually turned a heel as I talked, which I felt was something, though nobody else noticed it. Lady Oxford was a great personality; she just hated the war and I wish I had met her again. She was a most brilliant conversationalist.

Spring came slowly. The spring would be the acid test, we felt, and if we got through this we should be all right; it was to be now or never, we told one another. Goodness, how many springs we were to feel that way!

April 1st, 1940

They say the war is now about to start. It has been a glorious spring day and Mabel Constanduros dined here.

April 8th, 1940

We have mined Norwegian waters, which I think is a good idea and only hope it gives Hitler the headache it gave me!

April 9th, 1940

Something of a shock after all my jubilations yesterday, for apparently Hitler hasn't a headache after all. He has just taken Norway and Denmark, and I'm the one with the headache.

April 15th, 1940

We have landed a B.E.F. in Narvik. The Canucks, I understand, but news is so difficult to get, and more difficult to believe when we do get it.

April 25th, 1940

Now for the pain-in-the-neck budget. It's tough. Postage 2½d. Postcards up to 2d. Super-tax from £1500 a year, and that's got me, curse the cards! Still, it's worth it if it slaps Hitler. The bother is that far too many magazines are folding up, and that hits me, too. I wish I didn't worry so much.

May 4th, 1940

It is such a lovely day, and I went for a long walk in Regent's Park with the trees just out. Our Norwegian exploits are the most ghastly flop, I believe, and now we are all over the place again.

May 6th, 1940

The *Afridi* gone, and one French and one Polish destroyer. The news gets grimmer every day, I think this spring is the nastiest that I have ever known. Chamberlain seems to be for it to-morrow in parliament, and privately I am most hideously depressed.

May 8th, 1940

There seems some fearful dispute in parliament, and they are voting tonight. Chamberlain may be out yet. (I bet he won't be. Parliaments work in such strange ways.) Things are very black and all along everything seems to have been badly bungled.

Neville Chamberlain was a very sick man, and he must have seen the red light coming with dying eyes. It was more and more evident that from the time he had predicted permanent peace we had taken this war far too easily, and a bill would be presented for our indolence which would perhaps be paid in the lives of men. On May 9th Chamberlain's position was worse.

May 9th, 1940

Val Gielgud and I lunched together discussing future plays, a form of work I enjoy enormously. It is again one of those too beautiful spring days, and it almost seems that Chamberlain will have to retire. Everything is working up to a climax very fast indeed.

It came all at once, for next day, when I was lunching at the Ivy with Collie Knox, he told me that even as we were eating *hors d'œuvres* Winston Churchill was at the Palace with the King and now everything would be quite different.

'But isn't Mr. Churchill the impetuous kind, and as yet untried?' I asked.

'You're wrong,' said Collie. 'Churchill is the one man who can win this war for us, and thank God we are going to get him.'

Only that very morning the postman, a bit of a chatterbox, had brought the news that Hitler had invaded Holland and Belgium.

'Lord! That's coming near home,' said Robbie.

'I'll say it is! What does it mean?'

'It means there's a war on.'

I rang up the *Daily Mail* and had a word with Cecil Hunt (the fiction editor), who said that unhappily the postman was quite correct. He thought that things must be awful over there, and the Queen of Holland's life was in danger; he said that both she and Princess Juliana had been shot at. He understood that parachutists had been dropped, all equipped with machine-guns and collapsible bicycles. ('They think of everything, don't they?') But nobody knew as yet how bad it really was.

When I looked into the sky I thought that the balloon barrage had been strengthened. Later that day my headache became so unbearable that I collapsed, tried to pull myself together, but failed.

May 15th, 1940

Event is following event in the most bewildering way. All the time war comes closer, and the Dutch have thrown in their hands. They say that Brussels is likely to fall this week.

May 16th, 1940

Things are becoming very serious, and as far as I can see we have nothing with which to stop this onrush of the enemy. Mr. Churchill is in Paris. I have felt so dreadfully ill all day with this headache that I am nothing but a nuisance and could weep for shame. I feel now that when I leave London tomorrow it will be for ever.

The dreadful memories of my previous adventures as an evacuee haunted me, but we went down to Cirencester for a while, for it had a good train service up and down for Robbie and I could stay at the Fleece.

I don't know whether this was wise at this particular time. My father thought that I should have stayed on in London, but I was feeling so terribly ill and the headaches were so paralysing, and almost daily, that I had to get away. Every morning I woke to fresh agony, groping to get the Femergin injection, and trying not to groan as I waited for it to work. That would be an hour in hell.

Pip had been a student at the Royal Agricultural College, which meant that I knew people in Cirencester, and it was also something of a backwater from the war.

The Dutch royal family had come over here. Prince Bernhardt had been seen at Liverpool Street station helping the nurse with the carry-cot in which his second baby Princess Irene lay. Princess Juliana looked dazed, the Queen utterly exhausted.

At Cirencester the war news got worse.

May 21st, 1940

Arras and Amiens have fallen, and I now feel that the Germans must win. Isn't it shocking? Their strategy seems to have been wonderful, whatever is said, and although everybody insists that the French must hold on (after all they have the Maginot Line), as far as I can see they are collapsing. It's so annoying how men won't admit this sort of thing before women, when all the time the women know as well as they do.

I dined one night with Dr. Grove-White and a last-war colonel friend of his. At nine o'clock they turned on the news—

a bad mistake!—and it came through more disheartening than ever. When it was over there was a very nasty silence.

'You don't think the French are ratting, do you?' the doctor asked. The colonel was plain-spoken.

'It wouldn't be new for them if they did. Last time, you know, and I bet they do it again. Blast the Froggies.'

'If they do rat, what . . . ?'

The old colonel looked round him with the light of war in his eye. 'We won last time and we'll damn' well win this. All I hope is that we never have to fight cheek to cheek with those flipping French again. They've no knowledge of the Queensberry rules.'

'What's this business about a bulge?' the doctor asked. 'What's happened to the Maginot Line? They made enough fuss about it once; you don't suppose anybody has found a hole in it, do you?'

None of us knew and 'the Bulge' was the subject of conversation everywhere at this time. What was it? What could have happened? What did a bulge mean?

The three of us walked back to the Fleece through the exquisite May evening with the stars, and I knew then that we waited for the miracle. Only that could save us. That miracle was granted to us at Dunkirk (that is something in which I shall always believe), but it was to be a long road home from that moment.

Robbie came down for a week's leave and very welcome he was. Leaving Cirencester we went to Bath to stay, which is the most charming and the most unwarlike city we have. The R.N. was there, so we were amongst old friends. The peaceful elegance of Bath is in itself good medicine for a perturbed soul, and most certainly the old city helped me find peace at that dangerous time.

The French communiqué said, 'It grows hourly graver,' and nobody contradicted this, bulge or no bulge. I talked to a young R.N. wife with two babies and asked what she would do if

France fell and we were invaded. It looked that way. She said rather than let the babes be brought up as nasty little Nazis she would get poison and finish them. Many felt the same way. Most mothers insisted that this would be a personal duty, if . . .

On May 28th, when we were breakfasting in the hotel above the Botanical Gardens, there came the radio news that King Leopold of the Belgians had surrendered. We were completely horrified. I remembered an old Etonian who had fagged for him at school telling me he had never tipped his fags properly, and end-of-term treat had been half a stale currant loaf and no cake! It is shocking what one remembers when a crisis comes.

That morning Robbie and I walked down the hill to 'elevenses' at Fortt's, which is something of a ceremonial in Bath. Nobody there was worried. We sat down to a large table with several friends, and one of the girls said: 'I put my money on Belgium. They'll hold the fort like they did last time and save the show; good, gallant little Belgium.'

'But they've thrown in the towel already,' said Robbie, who has a positive genius for breaking bad news abominably.

You could have heard a pin drop in Fortt's!

If it hadn't all been so frightening it would have made me laugh, for apparently nobody had bothered to listen to the radio that morning; now they got the real shock of their lives. All those gaping faces over their silly buns were a sight that I shall never forget. The diary gives my real feelings as that evening I looked out of the hotel bedroom window, across the deep bowl in which Bath lies, clasped by the surrounding hills.

May 29th, 1940

I cannot believe that there will be three more years in this five-year diary of mine. Everything seems to be conspiring against us, and the Huns coming on. In France there is complete chaos and no respect for civilians, none even for the poor little children. The B.E.F. can surely never get out of this alive.

Yet in wartime we move in a quick and a mysterious way. I wrote again on the 31st:

May 31st, 1940

B.E.F. almost evacuated. We didn't deserve this, I know, and all I hope is that we learn the lesson from it. . . . Our little boats did the job, half the old non-seaworthies from Margate, Whitstable and the Cinque Ports tottered out to sea, and never did England boast of a finer fleet. May we remember what they did!

The next day when I was walking in Milsom Street I saw the most inspiring sight. It was outside Fortt's that the royal car appeared, and out of it got a lord-in-waiting and trotted inside. Queen Mary, the very spirit of a country that we hoped would never die, sat there erect. In a moment out came the lord holding between two fingers a neat little bag of the famous Bath buns. It looked absurd! Yet somehow so impressive, though maybe that is the wrong word to use, but the Queen Mother had about her something that was more than majesty. She was the woman who would never give in. We knew that.

With the morning we returned to London.

*   *   *

I was horribly conscious of my own inability to do anything that would really help the war, and, goodness, how much I wanted to do something! This feeling of helplessness possessed me. It was destroying to be aware of a physical weakness, a driving pain which held me back when every single person was wanted so much.

As soon as I got to London I went over to Balham to see my father and Jo. He was busy with a book, a register of medical practitioners in Harley Street from early days, and getting great pleasure from it. I felt that for a man who would be eighty next

December the capital was not where he should be, for I had little doubt that Europe would be conquered. I tried to persuade him to go home to Stratford-on-Avon but he was most unresponsive. He'd wait, said he, he'd hate to miss the fun.

'But if the B.E.F. flops out we could lose the war,' I reminded him.

'Oh no,' said he, 'we've never lost a war yet, and I'm not saying this because I'm old and silly. There is a destiny that shapes our ends, put your money on that. A man like Hitler is bound to make some colossal mistakes. It's bred in him.'

'He hasn't done too badly to date.'

'I know, and it's because we have made some cracking mistakes, too. Now we have someone out of the top drawer in power, and we needed that. Winston is a fighter. I daresay the top drawer sounds snobbish and out of date, but it has the guts to go on when lots of lower drawers shut up.'

I thought of Queen Mary sitting in the car waiting for her buns for tea. Maybe my father *had* something there.

When we got home the telephone was ringing madly, for Robbie was wanted. The sudden news came that some of the Foreign Office Communications Department were to go down to Bucks—all very hush-hush of course—and we had to give up the flat and go down there to live. This was stampede. It was irritating because we had just renewed our lease for three years on the flat, and war or no war a lease is a lease. Jockeyed out of it, we should have to pay. Oh hell! said I.

This was perhaps the greatest week in the history of England. It was full of mystery, of strange rumours, of wholly unbelievable facts, and of women and children being machine-gunned along the roads of France. Death spattered those roads; ditches were choked with rotting bodies, everything lay before the hideous scything of the victorious Reich.

The major part of our army was being taken off, the little boats game to the last plodded to and fro. Guy Meysey-Thompson, husband of Betty Hand, the editor of *Woman's*

Friend, told me later, 'It was like the worst thunderstorm that I have ever known.' Trainloads were coming through Kent to be met at every station by the untiring W.V.S. with tea, with cakes, and a blessing.

At the right hour a mist had come over the sea, and in that mist many escaped who otherwise would have died. And then they say this is not the age of miracles! Just before we left the maid brought in her returned young man for a drink. In that hour any man who had survived Dunkirk was a hero and it was an honour to receive him. He told us how shocking it had been, every man crawling on, and for himself, but he was convinced that if we had the right equipment, and in particular tommy-guns, we could fight them on their own ground and beat them.

We knew that all the English signposts were being removed, and milestones dug up, so that if the Huns did land they wouldn't know where they were. Or so we hoped. Also, delivery vans had their addresses and telephone numbers deleted.

'But,' I said, 'supposing they have fitted themselves out with some of our Ordnance maps? It's possible.'

We'd gone pretty well potty, I felt.

June 6th, 1940

The next great battle of the war started on the Somme yesterday. O God, do give us another miracle, and what can be happening to the poor French civilians in all this? And those little children, some wounded and lying by the roadsides?

I said to Robbie as we planned our departure, 'What do we do with the fish?' For I had kept Japanese tri-tails for some time in the radio niche in the wall.

'They're coming with us, of course,' said he, 'nothing would make me part with my fish.'

On the Sunday we raised the petrol from an unknown source —very hush-hush—and went off. On the way we picked up

Bozo (Mr. George Antrobus, senior King's Messenger), who was a darling. He dressed like a scarecrow, looked eccentric, was madly interested in railways, and was a charmer. That sounds peculiar, but it is true. There was nowhere to live in the actual town, so we arranged with a hotel in Buckingham *pro tem.*, then sat down to tea in the lounge before returning home.

It was there that I heard one of Winston Churchill's famous and inspiring speeches which spurred me on. Soon, it seemed, the Huns who had trampled Europe underfoot would be at our heels, for this was indeed a crazed world. We *had* to win, and as yet he had nothing to offer save blood and tears and toil and sweat.

At night one lay awake thinking of the barren beaches where still too many waited to be taken off, and some of them would never be saved. Of too many women mad with anxiety, and of the children who were already orphaned. But this was war, and war *isn't* wonderful.

3

But war's a game, which, were their subjects
wise, Kings would not play at.

COWPER

WE LEFT the flat that evening.

Robbie went to fetch the car from the Colebrook Garage, and I waited sitting on the suitcase I had packed amid tears, and which was the only piece of furniture in the bedroom that Gilbert Frankau had liked so much. A tiny portable wireless was at my side giving me hourly details, which were horrifying. It must be so much easier if one is born without the power to think for oneself; without perception as to what may lie ahead, without imagination—my inspiration and my curse!

Starting from London I took off a cornflower-blue hat and tipped it on to the back seat, not noticing that it had gone into the goldfish tank! When I did look round I was horrified to see that the water had turned to indigo! This was at Amersham, and we had to pull into a hotel yard and humbly ask if we could change the goldfish water! They thought us mad; we rather thought we *were* mad.

Dismally we came to Buckingham.

On Midsummer Day the French signed with Italy at 6.35 in the evening, which meant their war ended that night. The unknown danger drew closer. All the week in hot blazing weather people discussed what they would do if . . . and suddenly even the fields of England became unfriendly. We knew only too well what had happened to the French refugees, and the death roll there. Nobody had a shadow of doubt that our people would share that fate, if not worse, for Hitler hated us in particular and would be out for vengeance; for we had snatched back our men from under his very nose at Dunkirk.

That night we went to bed with sick hearts, and I must have been fast asleep when the air-raid siren went. This time I had a pretty good idea that this was the real thing. The French finished, to hell with England! We went downstairs with gas-masks and into a cellar which had been made into an unsafe shelter. There were cobwebby bottles everywhere, a poor light, and I thanked heaven that I had brought my knitting with me, but wished people would not keep saying that everyone knew the place to be haunted. We were all calm, perhaps even more so because nothing happened, and we were there from a quarter to one till four in the morning, when the all-clear blasted its way through.

I went upstairs and drew back the bedroom curtains.

The dawn was in the sky—pearl and pink-topaz, one of the most beautiful dawns that I have ever seen—and looking at it I realized that this was the doorway to a new world. The square in Buckingham looked brilliant, and the A.R.P. wardens were walking about. They had brought out horse-boxes, believing they would be useful if we had a lot of casualties. Not a bomb had dropped within earshot.

Robbie was already asleep, but somehow I could not go to bed, for I felt that this moment was momentous, and I stayed at the window looking out at the gathering glory of that dawn, and feeling that while there was this abundance of beauty surely it could in the end conquer hideousness? Or was I being silly?

Something must happen soon, I thought. *It did!* Here is the entry in the diary:

June 25th, 1940

In the air raid shelter from 12.45 to 4, but no bombs fell as far as I know. Today Robbie got the sack. This is the most mysterious thing that ever happened, for in this vital hour of our history the most secret department of the Foreign Office has gone mad. I wish I could shoot Lord Halifax. I never liked his face much, but what he and his are doing to the 'Silver Greyhounds' is quite unbelievable. We go home tomorrow.

What had happened was this.

Robbie was in the Communications Department, where messages to and from all over the world were put into or translated from code and cypher. The whole department suddenly received a month's notice from the head of the Foreign Office, Sir Alexander Cadogan. They were told that other jobs would be found for them with equal salary and conditions, but they had to stay on another month, then a third, because—and God be thanked for that—they could not train others for the job in any shorter time.

In this department were the King's Messengers, valued men known to outsiders as the 'Silver Greyhounds'. Bozo, the senior, had been there well over twenty years.

Nothing could be done about it.

This was the most shattering case of stark injustice and

D

dismally inept running of an office that I had ever heard of, but I could not help because the papers were censored.

At this tragic moment the Foreign Office was at an impasse. Cyphering is not easily learnt. In the place of about two dozen men they took on over a hundred and fifty Post Office employees in their most secret department, and all of them youngsters. I almost lost touch with the war I was so furious.

We made a miserable journey back to London, fish and all, booking in at the same hotel in South Kensington where we had lived before the flat. Casually I write in my diary next day:

June 27th, 1940

Robbie took me to see *New Faces* again because I needed cheering up, he felt. I only wish a nightingale would sing in Berkeley Square. How wonderful Judy is in this! Everybody says that Hitler will start his war on us about July the second.

It was as casual as that! 'Is the war starting here this week?' 'No, I understand it is down for Thursday on the following week.' That was our angle.

In the middle of it all I collapsed again, with even worse headaches, and who could wonder? The evening papers had got the rumour that there were flat-bottomed boats off Holland, and King Carol had gone over to the Axis. It was a bewildering war.

Recovering a little I went out to lunch with Michael Joseph in Greek Street, eating in a funny little restaurant with good food, I must say. He told me that by this day month we should be fighting at least thirty miles inland in England. I was so sorry that I had ever gone out with him.

One thing was certain and that was that it helped being in surroundings I trusted and knew. These things are vital in wartime. A number of French officers had come over and were staying with us at the hotel. General de Gaulle was in and out a lot and never seen without his hat! Life was becoming such a daze that we had no idea what was actually happening, and it was then that Robbie was appointed as a censor in the Ministry of Information. The hours were appallingly long, twenty-four on duty, twenty-four off, so in that way the whole rules of regular sleep were uprooted. But this appointment did mean that at a time when I was desperately ill he would be here with me.

'I'm lucky,' I said, 'but where is this war getting us? What are we fighting for?'

'Principles,' he told me.

'We shall be invaded, of course?'

'Obviously.'

'And then?'

'There's always the Royal Navy.'

'Yes, but—will it . . . ?'

'Undoubtedly,' said he firmly.

One ought to be tremendously stirred at being married to a naval officer who has this fatih. He should never have retired— my wretched health did that for him and I'll never forgive it. I wonder why I had to be so interminably ill? Perhaps in the pre-birth period I put my money on a too-expensive face and re-trenched on the works. If that was so it is a mistake that I shall not repeat.

★   ★   ★

I managed to do some work with the War Savings Certificates at Harrod's, and twice received the Duchess of Kent for them. The first time I took her round a deadly dull exhibition and felt very sorry for her in this because she must have been bored stiff. She was kind, not effusive, but tried to be interested, and I sympathized. I had my own Silver Bullet collection there, asking people to put money into an enormous silver bullet to buy a shot with which to hit back. The already falling bombs in southern England helped this, and when an air-raid started, and the planes were overhead, we went the rounds with a tin helmet (other way up of course) and did quite well.

For now the Huns were at hand.

Picnickers were machine-gunned in amiable Sussex. People taking tea in the home garden were suddenly shot up. They were not dismayed, they adopted the English angle on such a situation. They were just 'opping mad. Blackberrying children were potted at from the skies, and Sussex became a quite dangerous place in which to live; and all the while we waited for the invasion to start, because of course it simply must come.

August 2nd, 1940

Hitler's planes scattered leaflets last night in Southampton and Bristol and South Wales. They were headed '*A Last Appeal to Reason*', and they were accepted gaily and now are being sold at a bob a nob for the Red Cross. Only the English could do this and with such glee. People are talking about something that they call the Battle of Britain though none of us really know this is on. Planes are everywhere and every now and then bombs pop down. It's warming up.

We were on the edge of one of the greatest battles of our history; years later we were told that it was now that we won the war! Yet on the face of things life was moderately normal, one could hardly believe that something was happening.

August 10th, 1940

I took my father along to the Zoo this afternoon, which he rather likes, and in the evening we went to see the '*Dream*' in Regent's Park. It was very pleasant and Robert Atkins pleased to see us. We had a long talk afterwards.

August 12th, 1940

After supper I went along to see Collie Knox in his lovely new home in St. Leonard's Terrace, Chelsea. You could not believe that there was a war on, save that an enormous barrage balloon was 'at anchor' in Burton's Court opposite. Collie is so brave, a soldier through and through, I am not brave at all. If I can't fight I sulk, and I'm not getting much of a fight out of this war.

Tonight hundreds of our planes have gone over to Germany, it was a wonderful sight, but how will they get back again?

August 13th, 1940

They say our men brought down 63 Nazi planes yesterday and fifteen already today. There are enormous aerial battles going on along the coast which could easily be the start of an invasion, for we know Hitler's barges are waiting for this. Pip is stationed at Exeter with the R.A.F. (ground staff) and he says I'd be surprised at the fun and games.

August 14th, 1940

Seventy-eight planes down yesterday.

August 15th, 1940

The air-raid siren went whilst I was lunching with Constance Holt (editor of *Woman's Own*) in her fifth floor flat. *Not* the safest place! Today is the one when Hitler predicted that he would be crowned in London (I *don't* think). Constance and I talked war whilst waiting to be bombed, but apparently the raid was over Croydon and not here at all. 90 planes down today.

August 18th, 1940

It is very hot indeed and as we started hotel lunch the siren went.
There was an awful buzzing sound but no bombs. It all began
again at five when I was at work, so I took the book down into the
shelter which has the steam heating pipes in it, and a glass roof in
places. (However did they pass it?) Old Mr. Fisher was there
alone and shaky, and had a heart attack. (This was not my charm,
but something went off with a boom just as I arrived.) It's a good
thing I was a V.A.D. in World War No. 1, because I'm starting
it all over again with Mr. Fisher in World War No. 2. 'You're
quite all right. Don't worry. I'm here and I'll see after you,' and
all that stuff. . . .

*   *   *

From now on we went from warning to warning all day and
all night. The effect it had on poor Mr. Fisher was the constant
attack and I was very sorry for him. We spent most of the nights
in the basement shelter with the steam pipes and the glass roof. It
was fairly empty till the sirens went, then the crowd came
surging down into it. One night Robbie took me out into the
area to look at the shrapnel popping on the street and it was quite
exciting. The Huns had now produced a most hideous screaming
bomb which gave people the willies, because they could hear it
coming down and had only to wait for the bang. Hearing it
made everyone think, 'This is for me!'

In the shelter one played Patience when things were bad, or
knitted or dozed or read, but I decided that these uncomfortable
conditions could not go on for ever. We sat in deck-chairs, which
I have never liked, and I determined to get something better on
which to sleep.

One day I went to John Barker's in a taxi. Just as we stopped
in Kensington High Street the siren began, and at this stage the
ruling was that every shop immediately locked its doors and that

was that. I got out of the taxi and saw a completely empty street, with the shrill of the wardens' whistles and a veritable thunder from the sky. I looked up and for the first time saw what I believe was called a dog-fight.

In this war you did not know whether to dive into a doorway and perhaps get the lot down on you, or stand in the street with the shrapnel popping, say a prayer, and leave the rest to the Almighty. It was *His* pidgin, anyway.

The raid was brief and the moment the all-clear went John Barker's opened their doors and in I went, to buy two most satisfactory mattresses for ourselves to put on the floor of the shelter. I got a porter to carry them out and beckon to a taxi for me in the High Street, only to find that he was deaf and dumb; and just as he and I got out with the mattresses on a barrow, off went the siren again! We were exactly where I had been only half an hour ago, with the additional liability of one deaf-and-dumb man and a couple of bulky mattresses.

This time it was a much longer raid, and we must have looked fairly silly standing there, whilst the poor man had no idea of what was going on, and it was not within my power to tell him. In the end the all-clear came and the doors reopened, and I and my mattresses got into a taxi and I was bowled off to South Ken. before I was caught yet again.

This, thought I, undoubtedly *is* the Battle of Britain.

My encouraging son wrote that it would get worse, and now we lived from one air raid to the next and asked no questions as to the possibilities of the future. The first time I was in a public shelter was in Battersea Park, where I had been walking, with my gas-mask, in which was slipped knitting, a bar of chocolate (which I daren't eat lest I could never get another), and two aspirin. Like this all emergencies were catered for. The gunfire was noisy, though nothing dropped, but the people in the shelter were so wonderful. We exchanged knitting patterns, then when the all-clear went shot home before the next siren.

August 31st, 1940

It has been an all-night raid and we are now starting the fifth one today which makes my twenty-sixth. I am sick of wanting sleep and have now decided that I'll ignore the damned things, and if I'm hit, I'm hit.

★   ★   ★

It was burningly hot weather, the thermometer in the eighties, and still we were waiting for the invasion which did not come. We had passed from the interminable cold war, when nothing had ever happened, into a phase when everything happened, and countries fell before the force of the Axis with a desperate crash, whilst we waited only for our turn to come. Germany had reached the other side of the 'little moat' which had somewhat upset Napoleon's plans, and which we hoped might upset Hitler's too. Most of our equipment had been left behind in France, we knew that. I imagine that Dunkirk must have become a proper depot for old iron, and now we had the Home Guard, immensely willing but apparently unarmed. They constituted much of our army.

They say old soldiers never die. It's true.

There came rumours that something had happened; they grew. It was said the Germans had started an invasion and it had been repulsed, that it was an almighty victory, and instantly the rumour was squashed. No one must say anything. It wasn't true anyway. Here are my diaries at the time of the alleged invasion.

September 15th, 1940

Now we have had 77 raids. The machine guns keep on going all around us. Bombs fell over London today and one might almost think something special was on the *tapis*, for there was such a to-do. They mucked up Buckingham Palace a night or two ago.

Meanwhile we are living in and out of this dratted cellar and Mr. Fisher is having an awfully tough time, poor lamb!

September 16th, 1940

Five more raids, and a really ghastly one last night with those horrifying screaming bombs; they were so bad that our second chef died from shock in the shelter alongside ours. It *is* unnerving, but worst of all is the fact that we live like rats. Some people never go upstairs even for the most natural reasons, but use the coal bins, which I think is a bit steep. This is a ghastly phase.

Yet in those twenty-four hours the future of the war had been decided, and the strangest gossip was going the rounds. They even said that we had fallen back on the old trick when invasion threatened and had set the sea on fire.

Later my son told me much.

This story has been denied: he was in it; I met three pilots later on who had also been in it; and I believe it to be true. For the preceding week the staff at Exeter had known that something was up. Pilots and crews actually slept in their planes, and lived and ate in them. At the time there were only fifteen planes at Exeter and they wanted more most desperately. Pilots were grounded for want of them, using the most rude language and tearing their hair.

Suddenly every living person was called in on the job, even the canteen staff were helping to load the belts, every single pair of hands they could find was dragged into it, and nobody could stop even for food. They were fighting for their lives, and for ours as well. A lion had bared her teeth, and if she were mangy, as they thought, she had something in her that spat back hell.

News had come that the invasion barges along the French coast were pushing off for England.

Our planes were going to and fro all the time, wasting never a moment in pursuing the prearranged plans. The fighters went out at speed and sprayed the sea with petrol. The bombers went out after them and dropped their incendiary bombs, and in an instant the sea was on fire. Further planes followed and machine-gunned any who lived. They swept the sea. A Sergeant Pilot landing for refuelling said to my son: 'That ought to teach the b——'s we don't want 'em! They'll never do that agin, blast 'em.'

Later I knew from friends along the coast-line that numbers of German soldiers were washed up, twenty and thirty at a time. I believe this story to be true; for I find it hard to credit that a madly obstinate man like Adolf Hitler would not have attacked in some way or other, even if our air force had previously given him a licking in the air. I am sure he was mad enough to do this, and that the reaction of 'the few'—and nobody will ever know how those young men fought—saved us from annihilation.

Later on when my son was employing a German prisoner-of-war on his farm, a man not a Nazi who was willing to talk about much, he asked him about that day. The man went white and said it was too dreadful to speak of. It had been the deepest villainy and the death those men had died had been too shocking. He would talk of anything else, but never of that. Spain drank once from that same cup—'Time enough to finish the game and beat the Spaniards too'—Germany had tasted its bitterness, I am sure.

Earlier on—September 7th—news came that the London docks were on fire. Robbie coming home early thought we ought to go and have a look after supper, for we were still treating the war as some amusement on which you didn't have to pay entertainment tax. That is the British spirit. We went to Westminster Bridge and when we got there saw exactly nothing save a copperish glow in the direction of the City. That was when the sirens went. We tried to get into St. Stephen's Dive, but the old routine of every door shutting on one in one's agony barred us out, and in the end we went into a public air-raid shelter in

Parliament Square, which was *not* the best place in which to spend a raid.

The people were quite wonderful and we sat talking whilst bombs dropped around us, and over our heads those brave young gentlemen of Johnny Pegler's army were losing their lives to defend their country as in 1914–18 their fathers had done before them at Mons and on the Somme.

It became bedlam, then about eleven it seemed to be cooling a little and we decided that we would make one of those quite frightful dashes for home. We sneaked out, took a deep breath, then hand in hand galloped off for St. James's Park Underground station. The trouble with that place was that it was not sufficiently underground, but we left it at exactly the right moment, for four minutes later it got a direct hit. 'We do miss them, don't we?' I said to Robbie.

When we got to South Kensington station there was that eternal problem of how did we find out how the world was going on upstairs? We stayed below for a while but it was very dull, then Robbie went up and came back saying it really wasn't at all bad, and perhaps the worst was over. The next moment we were dashing up Old Brompton Road, hand in hand as ever, where the sandbags jutting out provided eternal danger points; and we hurled ourselves through the swing doors of the hotel at the identical second that an almighty bomb dropped a few yards behind us, and this propelled me forward at speed. One minute I was in the swing doors saying 'Oh!', the next found myself buffeted against the porter's desk on the far side saying 'Blast!'

The porter said: 'There, there, madam. Well I never!' in the way the English accept these variations of wartime fate. He was not disheartened.

September 19th, 1940

Seven really nasty raids today which makes the lot 94 so far, and the most ghastly night of them all. My poor old father got a delayed action bomb in the next door garden and is an evacuee. This has upset me dreadfully for he is very brave and so is Jo, poor frail little piece that she is, and both are far too old to be submitted to the war. But can I persuade them to get out of it, I wonder?

My father had rung me up just before breakfast telling me in a pitiably quavering voice that the street had been cleared and he and Jo bustled into a shelter in their night clothes where they had been since five in the morning. Now the bomb had exploded, he understood, and half the houses in Ryde Vale Road had collapsed with it, his amongst others. He had only what he stood up in, and began to cry. What did he do? It was far too much to expect any man of eighty, or thereabouts, to endure. I asked if he could get a taxi, and he could. I told him to come straight to me as they were and I would fix up hotel accommodation for them. Our place was full, but I got another a few yards up the street. When they arrived they were in dusty dressing-gowns, both crying bitterly and obviously needing food. I took them along, put them to bed, and they had breakfast at once. I just hated the Germans for this —hitting the old is a bit too much, they are so helpless.

I suggested they slept a bit—they were almost safe for the moment—whilst I went out and bought some clothes. They did sleep, the best thing for them, and I well aware of a tremendous responsibility did my best.

Late that afternoon I went down to Balham with Robbie, and we crawled into the wrecked house to bring back what I could find. The anxiety was that all the doors and windows being blown out any looter or thief could get in. It was shocking to see the familiar objects of my childhood exposed to every Tom, Dick, and Harry (at this stage looting was *the* thing!), and the police had far too much to do to be a real help.

In the next air raid and the comparative quiet of our shelter I wrote to Edith, once a parlourmaid at the Rectory, to ask if she living in Stratford knew of anyone who could take in Dad and

Jo. Anyway, *pro tem*. I suppose at heart I must have known that it would be for the rest of their lives, but I had to get them out of this as quickly as I could, and where I thought they would be least lonely. Within a week I had taken rooms for them, driven them to Paddington station, and sent them off. I felt that Stratford would be tolerably safe. It would be one of the last places to be bombed, because if Ribbentrop wanted to live in the Tregenna Castle at St. Ives (he had said that he did), I imagined that Buckingham Palace in London with Shakespeare's birthplace as a country house might be ideal for Hitler.

When he finally beat England. . . .

If . . .

★   ★   ★

It was futile to do nothing during the raids, and they had come for good. I realized that far too many of the older people were badly frightened and that they needed comfort. I managed to get some tea, for I had good friends in Ceylon who were assisting me, and I brewed this in the coal and coke bins which were alongside the actual shelter. My making tea there was a help in stopping the bins from being used for less sanitary purposes, and I felt that was a good thing. The servants went off duty, and around me were elderly people to whom a cup of tea meant something quite considerable, accompanied by something discreet such as, 'Not half as bad as last night, is it?' 'I think it's north of the park tonight, good luck to them.' 'Don't worry, they can't hit everybody, you know.'

I hated taking the tea-trays upstairs into the ground-floor lounge where people sat all night not realizing how hideously dangerous the big windows were. Whenever I emerged with the tray something frightful would drop—I got to expect it. I'd stand at the foot of those stairs, and say to myself, 'One, two, three, go,' and more often than not was very sorry that I *had* gone.

Cellar life was peculiar. We had forgotten the delicious feeling of sheets against the body, of lying in a comfortable bed. A friend went into Berkshire for the week-end and came back boasting that she had 'slept between real sheets!'. But every now and then it was too close to be pleasant. One lunchtime I was writing in the main lounge when I heard the whistling of one of those screaming bombs, ducked, and the next minute the dining-room windows went for six.

Food was abominable everywhere, and in the hotel we were really unhappy about it and signed a round robin hoping to get things changed. Apparently the powers-that-be had resented the fact that I made tea for people, attributed the round robin to me, and promptly asked us to leave. I think it was unfair, I had done a good deal for the place in my time, and if they had looked into the matter they would have found that the tea was inspired only by human sympathy.

I came to Cranmer Court again, for after all that was home, and this time I was coming back to it for ever. I managed to get a furnished flat which I could rent by the month. If Robbie was worried that I should have to spend every other night entirely alone in it, and anything could happen, that could apply to most people. My diary entries do not appear to have been over-anxious.

October 17th, 1940

We are back in Cranmer Court and had a better night though recently the raids have been dreadful. At the same time I am thankful to be in steel and concrete.

October 18th, 1940

I had a ghastly headache and could not even whisper for the pain was so bad. I'd an idea I'd die, but people don't die so easily. There was a shocking barrage last night, they have got something ew in Battersea Park, and shells were bursting all the time. I wonder who thinks that war is fun.

October 20th, 1940

The raids have been vile all day and night with no let-up. This has been a shocking week, and now there are unexploded bombs everywhere so that you cannot get into half the streets (always the ones you want). One comes to the dismal conclusion that there must be an end to it somewhere, but where can it be? And will the world after this be in the least like the world we knew before September of last year?

The horror of the attack on Coventry came, and my father wrote that he had watched it from the back garden in Stratford-on-Avon, from which he got a bird's eye view, and thought it was the most appalling thing that had ever happened. Bristol got it next. It looked as if this was the beginning—of what?

4

Cry, 'Havoc!'
WILLIAM SHAKESPEARE

WE ENTERED the second winter of the war; and where the first winter had been ice-cold in some strange bewildering peace of its own, this one was hot with bombs and was entirely a winter of war. Indeed we cried havoc.

Pip appeared out of the blue. The doorbell rang, and when I answered it there he was in Air Force uniform looking at me. There had been something of an upset, I never knew how it happened, but like so many of the modern young folks off he had gone; now I knew something terrible had taken place.

'Come in,' I said.

He had a broken marriage behind him and to the accompaniment of pom-poms, falling bombs, and the shriek of ambulance bells (all part of the backcloth to which I was rapidly becoming accustomed) I heard his story. I was not sure how Robbie would feel—a stepfather is sometimes less sympathetic about the prodigal son's return—and hearing his key in the door I shuffled Pip into the bedroom, just as a quite filthy bomb fell outside and both of us thought the windows were coming in. Then I went and explained the situation.

It was all right.

Next day Pip went round to see the sights. The curious thing was that the collapse of ancient buildings and the hideous chaos that was London now was treated as something visitors must at all costs be taken to look at. It was all part of the Cook's tour for the country cousin. Only the English can accept war this way, and win it as well.

St. Clement's had slumped into the Strand. The docks were blackened scars, with whole streets down, and wherever you looked there was some landmark of suffering and of courage and grim determination in a country struggling to win.

He stayed a couple of nights, a much more peaceful couple than we had had for some time, and he had not gone back five minutes before a real stinker began and I was all alone in the flat. That was the night of *the* egg, highly valued and saved as being a rare and luscious piece of food. *The* egg was to be my supper. I had it in a spoon and was in triumph conveying it to the waiting saucepan on the gas-ring when an enormous bomb fell and my egg went for six! I never saw it again. My head crushed on the oven, and my body black and blue from the fall, were as nothing compared to the dismal fact that I had lost *the* egg.

Bombs behaved mysteriously. That one had fallen in Shawfield Street, which is quite some way from us, yet it had deliberately selected *the* egg. The following morning, when I went to the Golden Bud in Sloane Street for elevenses, I was sitting at one end of a long sofa when a bomb fell, and instantly

E

I found myself sitting at the other end smothered in coffee. You never could tell with them. Anything could happen.

I had adopted the submarine H.M.S. *Ursula*, and knitted for them, sent them sheepskin jackets, magazines, everything that I could. They were most charming about it (till they went down) and wrote most friendly letters, and my one regret was that a year back I could have done so much more for them than was possible now. Everything was getting tighter.

As winter continued I sickened of the limitations of the furnished flat and decided to take a risk, rent an unfurnished one, and bring the furniture back from store. This was going to be a long war, probably longer than the last one, and the risk was worth while. At this time one could get one's pick of unfurnished flats at a reasonable rent, and I took one which looked out on to Chelsea Common, nowadays just a ragged bit of green with a rather dingy tree on it. We were to move in January.

December 19th, 1940

Today I saw a German aeroplane flying right under the balloon barrage, and so low that I recognized the crosses on its wings. That put me into something of a dither, and in my rage I spat at it and hit a dog.

I must have sunk low, but the bother was that week after week, with broken sleep, never out of a siren suit, and able only to snatch food or a bath when and as one could, told on human nature.

Christmas Eve, 1940

I have seen a miracle sight for there was a coster's barrow by Peter Jones's, with real lemons for sale. The first since the war. Not a glimpse of an onion as yet, but here's hoping. Last night

Churchill made a magnetic appeal to Italy on the radio. I don't suppose it'll do much good.

Brompton Oratory had its midnight mass at midday today, which is a precedent, I should think. Chocolate unobtainable.

Pip came home for a few days, and we were all very miserable because poor Bozo from the F.O. and his elderly father who was in the nineties were killed in a raid on Leamington.

December 29th, 1940

Simply hundreds of planes came over tonight, and they say it is the second great fire of London, for the whole city is ablaze. We saw little from here, but they could read by the light in the streets of Bloomsbury, and the stench of burning was appalling. Simpkin Marshall, Hodder, Ivor Nicholson and Watson, and Cassell's all went, and Sir Newman Flower manfully trying to save something. St. Bride's is a ruin, and one of our porters heard that Guildhall was down. Our lights all went out. The Austrian maid who is helping me in the evenings, when ours failed groped her way to me and said, 'It has refused.'

December 31st, 1940

Beaverbrook says that now we are only waiting for the invasion and it will for certain come this spring. For the moment Hitler is quieter, having set the city on fire, but goodness only knows what 1941 has in store for us. Whatever it is, it is safe to say that it couldn't possibly be nice. I feel utterly depressed about it all, my headaches at times unendurable, and now Pip is invalided out of the R.A.F. (something to do with his ears). He is to stay here so that I shall have someone with me at night, and now he has attached himself to an ambulance which he will drive through the raids. It sounds dangerous to me.

January 6th, 1941

Bardia fell to us yesterday, and I paid sixpence for one leek.
Sixpence! Think of that! Goodness, how that leek hurt me!
Bar chocolate seems to have gone and food is most awfully
difficult, so that during the week-end most of us had no meat
at all.

January 11th, 1941

One of those irritating raids with incendiaries everywhere, and
that included our courtyard, and on the roof, so we had fun.
More lemons have appeared for sale. Meat is the big difficulty.

Sunday, January 12th, 1941

I went a bust, hired myself a taxi and went round the burnt city.
It was far more dreadful than I had thought. I cannot imagine how
St. Paul's was saved, or how much life was lost. You can see right
through all the buildings that are left, Amen Corner truly
amen-ed. Ave Maria Lane—just gutted.

In the middle of January Robbie was sent up to Edinburgh for
the Censorship and would be away for a fortnight. I planned to
move during that time as a big secret, so that he would get no
worry with it. It was a dreadful move when it actually came to it,
with the days short and raids all the time. Blackout curtains were
always the major difficulty in those circumstances, but Pip and I
did it between us and were safely in with the furniture in place
the night before Robbie was due back. He would travel on the
Saturday night train, arriving at King's Cross about seven in the
morning when London would be black as pitch. Purposely I kept
the move secret, knowing he would go to the old flat, open the
door, and kiss the strange woman there thinking it was me! This
amiable little jest went wrong. The moment Robbie's taxi drew

up at the main entrance one of our porters told him where I was, and if ever there was a cad's trick, that was the one!

Robbie had come armed with food, for apparently in Scotland they hadn't got a clue about rationing. He had a rabbit when none of us had seen one for a year, some extra butter, and a string bag with eggs in it. These however had suffered something of a major disaster, for he, anxious to keep them safe, had hung the bag on a hook in the taxi roof, but turning a corner they had banged against the side and arrived dripping.

The snow had come.

London streets were calmly quiet with almost no traffic, and everywhere those hideous gaps where once proud buildings had stood. It was the first time I had ever recognized the fact that Piccadilly is quite hilly. With the strange inconsistency of human nature, I now longed for the noise of traffic, and the London I once had known, and I missed the crowds.

We all looked shabby, we should look much shabbier as the years went on, and the great cult of the hour was the string bag. These string bags had bounced back from the very beginning of the century and now were everywhere.

After the great fire of London the raids seemed to ease down somewhat, then with February they warmed up again, possibly with the thought of breaking us down before another shot at invasion. We always expected it. We waited for it; some said they would be glad to get it over, for anyway it had to come; others dreaded it.

Food was the major problem of every day.

February 20th, 1941

We can't buy any fruit of any kind, and they say jam is soon to be rationed. It is pathetic to see so many of the smaller shops closing down just because they cannot get the stuff to sell. Arding and Hobbs have however a marvellous tinned counter, and this actually includes honeycomb—the real sort! Last night the Huns picked on Chelsea as their 'target for tonight', and we had two sticks of bombs most unpleasantly close. You hear them popping along in your direction, each one coming nearer. Not funny!

March 1st, 1941

It's sickening that Hitler has said that March has always been his lucky month. Meat is so scarce, though so far meat, fats, sugar, and bacon are all that are actually rationed, though you can't get the other things for love or money. Meat is on allowance, 1s/2d a head for a whole week, and some weeks when they are particularly short those dratted butchers eke this out with bully.

March 7th, 1941

Carnations are 17s/6d a dozen, which is a thought, as I have never paid more than 6s/- a dozen before. Jam is to be rationed at the middle of this month and there is a ghastly rumour that it may only be 2 ozs. a nob per week. Eggs are maddeningly difficult because everywhere the fowls are being killed off, as food for them is unprocurable. Surely this is a poor outlook? Meanwhile we are busily preparing to be invaded and I have a nice little picnic bag ready for *the* week when nobody knows how things are going. Special leaflets are being issued with all particulars of what to do and when to do it. It seems to me that the reply to all queries, however, is *stay put and get on with your job*. Women of twenty and twenty-one are now to be called up.

It seemed almost curious that the crocuses could come out in Hyde Park in a world so vile, but the loveliest thing about flowers is their complete disregard of war.

I engaged a resident maid, Rosa, a middle-aged little Czech who had been here all twenty years, though I doubt if you would have thought so by her extraordinary accent. The raids were worsening.

*   *   *

Pip decided to give a party on March 8th, and because it seemed cowardly to admit that I did not want to go (I got a premonition of something odd) and not liking to show my anxiety, I went. It was to be for about eight of us, and at the Hungaria in the Hunter's Tavern. Pip had really wanted to take us to the Café de Paris, which was below stairs and therefore presumably safe, but when he rang up they were fully booked and he could not get a table.

We had not settled down in the Hungaria five minutes before a really frightful air raid started, and I don't think I had ever heard a noisier one. Undoubtedly they had their eye on Eros, Piccadilly Circus, and all that. The gypsy band were marvellous, and they played harder and louder in a wild effort to drown the row with Liszt. As the waiters worked I could see their faces growing tenser, their eyes almost frantic, and I began to get very nervous indeed but did not dare show it. The conversation between us all was now over-casual, trying to conceal what we really thought about it all.

When we arrived at the coffee stage Pip got restless, and thought that perhaps it would be a good idea to go across to the Café de Paris and dance there, so he went up into the hall to ring them up. When he returned his face was quite ashen.

He said: 'I say, there isn't a Café de Paris any more. The Huns got it five minutes ago, up there they are bringing in some of the wounded. It—it's pretty awful.'

Absurd as it may seem, I think that was the first time that it occurred to us, *It could be me*! In war one is very much inclined to treat the whole thing as some nasty dream, which one witnesses but in which one does not actually take part. Now there were two hundred dead and three hundred trapped.

We went upstairs.

The noise increased and now it had become like the worst express train going through Crewe station. A young girl in a white satin dress that was stained with blood sat in a corner staring hopelessly before her; a woman knelt beside someone on a stretcher.

None of these people seemed to be aware of any of us, only of a dreadful tragedy. Their eyes seemed to see nothing. There was blood everywhere. A man in a dinner jacket came in, an arm hanging limp and blood dropping on to the floor as he walked; he appeared to be quite unaware of it.

We waited until midnight and then there seemed to be a little lull, and Robbie grabbed my arm.

He said: 'Let's make a bolt for Piccadilly Tube. It's close, and we'd be far safer there. This place could go at any moment.' I did not want to leave Pip, or my cousin Leila who was with us, but he pulled me away. 'This is a case of every man for himself, you've got to come.'

So we went.

There were fire engines in the street, ambulances and the A.R.P. wardens everywhere. The sky was copper, and there was the constant crackle of flames in a building a few doors away. Worst of all was the terrible smell of burning, and of explosive, so bad that you could taste it, and against the horrid red glow the outline of distorted buildings, a single wall standing with sightless windows and through them disaster.

We took each other's hands and began running to the Tube entrance and far faster than I had believed to be possible. The noise was appalling, somewhere women were screaming, everywhere bombs were falling. Then, as we slithered down into the Tube and pelted for the escalator, all hell opened fire above us.

The moment we got right down that awful noise was deadened and in its place there came what was almost a phantom calm, horrid in its contrast. There was that sweet stench which comes to places where crowds sleep, and I began to retch. Bodies lay everywhere. The place looked like some battlefield (perhaps that was what it was) and the desolate attitudes of those who had lost heart struck me as being quite dreadful as I walked through them and over them. Yet in another corner a group were playing some card game, chattering as if this were a mere nothing, and chinking coins; in another a man sat on a kitbag playing a mandolin; I recognized the 'Eton Boating Song'—'What a place for that, and now!' I thought—whilst all the time the Tube trains lumbered through, came and went on their job.

We travelled to South Ken. I was beginning to feel the result of a night in the front line. One flops after having been faced with a hideous crisis, and then more when it is over. At South Ken. Robbie went up to see what things were like upstairs and I talked to the ticket collector.

A nice dismal Joe *he* was! 'They say this 'ere war'll last every bit of ten blarsted years,' he told me.

'Surely in ten years we shall all be dead?'

'I'll say! I 'eard Piccadilly Circus caught it tonight.'

'Yes, we've come from there. The Café de Paris got a frightful smack.'

He said, 'Ah!' and picked a tooth with one of his tickets. 'Funny thing, war!' he said. 'It works out this way, don't it?'

I got somewhat sick of his company and wandered along to the lift, and eventually Robbie came down again. He said that all things considered it was remarkably quiet upstairs, and he thought we ought to risk it. One has to take risks sometimes, sickening as they may seem to be, and if he had asked me I should have told him that the whole evening had been one big hell of a risk, but that was that!

It is a long way from South Ken. to Cranmer Court, and once we started it was a case of no return. We legged it down Pelham Street; something fell in the not too far distance just as we arrived at the Admiral Keppel, and for a moment I halted, but the Admiral Keppel looked to be most unfriendly, all locked and barred, and on we went. The all-clear sounded as we dashed into Cranmer Court.

Two hundred killed, three hundred trapped, was what I kept thinking. War is a most shocking thing.

★   ★   ★

The spring grew considerably more active.

The hotel we had lived in in Kensington had a bad night for, although not actually hit, the Indian restaurant nearby was, and blew in on them, and the people told me the appalling stink of curry was far worse than the smell of explosive.

Invasion coming closer I added to the box I called my invasion parcel, with its iron rations—a tin of tongue, one of butter, another of cheese, two jellies, a bag of flour to make bread with, and a fat tin of fruit. This was never to be touched at any cost, save when we knew that the Huns had landed, and we ourselves were in flight. Where we would fly to, I did not know. The leaflets said stay put. There are moments when one can *not* stay put and I wondered if the writers of the leaflets had considered this trifle.

The bother with rationing is that if you do manage to scoop some wonderful prize from under somebody's counter, or round at the back of a shop, you dare not eat it in case you can never get another. The problem was always *do* I eat it *now*? I kept a tin of ham four years this way and then lost it. We lived for four days on a goose's egg I had picked up and a very small tin of salmon. This was delicacy! But always one postponed the good meal for tomorrow. One had to.

After the revolution in Jugoslavia King Peter came to his mother's flat in Cranmer Court. Sometimes we saw them in air raids, when the bombs got near and glass was dangerous and we all went into corridors. The Queen was completely composed, however noisy it was outside; she just talked to her lady-in-waiting and never seemed to be worried. The King was almost amused. Once he brought with him a bottle of beer. On the whole, shelter life was a most peculiar form of existence when all hobnobbed together. One knitted. One read. One chatted in a low voice. But in the main one just hated every moment of it and prayed for the dawn to come. At that stage the daylight always seemed to make things considerably better.

During this time, and perhaps it sounds absurd to mention it, my great help, and the thing that composed me most, was the old prayer of my childhood which seemed completely suitable for this horror:

> Lighten our darkness, we beseech thee, O Lord;
> and by thy great mercy defend us from all
> perils and dangers of this night. . . .

Most times I was alone in the flat, trying not to listen and wondering what I'd do if I was hit, but perhaps it was unwise to think of that. One night it became so bad that both of us went into the corridor and parked down in a couple of deck-chairs. Beside Robbie was an oldish man and he snored so persistently that I went nearly mad with it. Never have I heard such trumpeting! Suddenly Robbie woke up, heard the row, took one look at the old man, picked up his own pillow, and hit the poor thing full blast in the face with it. Heavens, what a plonk that was!

It happened to be a very famous admiral, and just as I chokingly murmured, 'How's that for *lèse majesté*?' a bomb fell in the next street and took several of our windows with it.

*   *   *

'But how is all this going to end?' I wondered, 'because human nature cannot endure it much longer, and where are we going from here?' For a time the persistent rumour of Mussolini's assassination enchanted us, for one lived on rumours as though they sheltered us from our own calamities, which were numerous.

March 13th, 1941

We went down to see Collie Knox in his charming home at Ivy Hatch; how I envy him! We had tea in the garden and absolutely no fear of raids, wasn't that wonderful? I came home with some little onions, two hen's eggs and lumbago, but the latter was a mere nothing. March is too early for tea in the garden perhaps.

March 18th, 1941

Pip has got himself a flat in Chelsea Cloisters. Recently the barrage has been quite dreadful, they keep getting new guns and always more awful ones. I do not know how we continue in a world so noisy.

April 10th, 1941

Raids and more raids, and now three valuable generals have disappeared in Africa. The news is very alarming indeed, but perhaps if more generals disappeared we could win sooner. Admirals might feel the draught, too.

On the evening of April 16th we saw that another awful raid was coming, for the pre-attack planes were overhead, dropping the very pretty chandeliers of coloured lights which lit up everything and showed the way to the followers-up. Their beauty was a snare and a delusion, but they quivered over London in radiant colours, and looking out at them they seemed to represent an unreal Christmas night in a highly decorated sky.

Soon after, of course, the bombers came in to attack, my 569th raid, and this one was concentrated on Chelsea.

By midnight we deserted the bedroom and lay on the floor of the corridor in the flat, away from the danger of broken glass. Rosa refused to come out of her room, said she felt safer there and did not believe that the window could hurt her. In war the thing to do is to let people act as they feel safest.

In the next three hours sixteen land mines fell and all the bombs in the world. I do not think I can ever forget the horror of it, the frantic shock of not knowing what to do, or where to go, and almost wanting to be hit to get it over.

It must have been just before three in the morning when I had a sudden urge to lie down and go to sleep. Goodness alone knows why. I curled on to the floor outside the closed bathroom door, with Robbie at the far end of the corridor, knew nothing more until I tasted the acrid taste of explosive in my mouth and was brought round by the raucous sound of people screaming. Beside me in the hall, where the bathroom door had been before, was an enormous jagged hole, and the first thing I thought of was the Bruce Bairnsfather cartoon (1916) ('Who made that 'ole?' and Old Bill replying, 'Mice!').

Through this jagged gap, with a broken wall beyond it, I saw Cranmer Court across the back courtyard and it was on fire. The fire brigades had already arrived and had run up their ladders and were bringing people down. You would have thought that the fact that they had had time to get there would have warned me that I had been unconscious for some considerable time, but that apparently did not register.

('Who made that 'ole?' 'Mice!')

Then I heard Robbie calling, 'Ursula, Ursula?'

'I'm all right,' I said, but the blanket over me had become intolerably heavy, and I realized after a moment that it wasn't the blanket at all but the bathroom door, and most of the bath itself lying about me. Strangely enough I had not suffered a single scratch. 'Rosa?' I gasped. 'What about Rosa?'

Rosa was all right and came crying out of her shattered room full of glass. She complained only that she had lost the angel that her mother had given her years ago. She stood there crying and saying that she must have the angel. The fact that she was still alive did not impress her, the angel was her worry, and in the chaos and the darkness we could do nothing about it for her.

In spite of the fire in the far block ours was appallingly cold, with enormous holes in the outside walls, and all the time bombs were falling everywhere around us. Somehow now we hardly seemed to notice them, and I was confident that they never hit the same target twice. It isn't true, of course, but at that moment it reassured me considerably.

On the landing beyond the blown front door—which had completely disappeared—I saw the gas pilot-light burning. Imagining that this might warn the enemy, I advanced with what I considered to be heroism and solemnly turned it out, not realizing that the wing of Cranmer Court that was on fire was the target which any enemy might notice, and one little pilot-light was as nothing compared to it.

Two A.R.P. men came to satisfy themselves that no one was seriously hurt; they advised us to stay where we were, suggesting the linen cupboard as the safest shelter, that being the only place that had not been smashed. The three of us got into the very small linen cupboard and crouched there shivering in the cold, and feeling quite awful, not knowing what else to do. In the end Robbie went for a scrounge and found a bottle of crême-de-menthe rolling on the floor of the flat. He opened it with the idea of us all drinking it to get warm. Rosa wouldn't touch it. She started off one of her jabbers, and I have never met anyone who could jabber like Rosa when she was in that mood. A direct hit, the flat shattered, and one of our wings on fire, then to cap it all Rosa in a jabber; it was a bit too much. She was, she vowed, a non-alcoholic, and she would not touch drink. Even to be taken as medicine she would refuse it. She was icy cold and in the end I had to give her my coat and become the cold one, just because she would not touch the crême-de-menthe.

With the hard light of dawn and the raid still continuing, a young girl appeared in the shattered doorway. She wore no definite uniform, but an armlet, and I gathered that she was connected with the A.R.P. She took one look, then in an encouraging voice suggested that we could do better than this. She knew where we could get some hot tea and greater comfort and proposed taking us there. We climbed down the jagged stairs and twisted railings with her, and just as we got to the main door a bomb fell far too near for pleasure.

I said, I hope politely, 'Thank you so very much, but I rather feel there's no place like home.'

She wasn't having that.

She had firm hold of me and walked me along Whitehead's Grove now thick with glass, with brick-ends, and all manner of bits of the flats. She was amazingly cheerful. She discussed to-morrow's weather as though nothing unusual was afoot, was chatty about the sort of summer we might expect, and I could hardly believe that this was really happening. She took us into the centre block where Colonel Minshull and his pretty wife had a flat. Early in the evening they had had a hunch that this would happen, and were so convinced of it that they had prepared the flat: one room as a sort of dressing station, the other as a canteen. They were doling out tea and coffee, welcomingly and kindly, and in their flat the noise of the raid seemed to become gratify-ingly muted.

We sat there.

We seemed to be sitting there for hours, with Rosa still jabbering about her angel, and for the moment nothing could be done about her angel whatever she said. People came to the ever-open door; air-raid wardens, helpers, and the public. 'Have you seen Mrs. So-and-so?' 'Have you caught sight of Colonel What's-his-name?'

One strange old lady kept wandering up and down the corridor, but refused to come inside though we tried to persuade her to have some tea; she always fluttered off again. She was a poor little thing, very ill at ease, and Robbie who was now help-ing with the washing-up was worried for her. He said to a young soldier who was at the sink, 'There's a frightful little bag wander-ing to and fro and I think we ought to get her in here, for she doesn't quite know what she's doing.' The young soldier said: 'Oh, don't worry about her, she's always like that. It's my mother.'

With morning the all-clear came and we returned to the wrecked flat, which was unrecognizable. I found my clothes, then went down Sloane Avenue with the idea of going to Chelsea Cloisters, where my cousin Leila lived, and getting a bath there. As I walked up the street I suddenly realized that I wasn't normal. I wore a siren suit and carried my clothes under one arm, whilst with the other hand I swung a girdle by a suspender. I was singing. I imagine I looked dotty.

The bath I got at Leila's was apparently full of broken glass, but nothing bothered anybody after that night; we had experienced sharper episodes than that one. My one worry was that the scattered concrete dust had turned my hair completely grey and I could *not* get it clean again.

I was dressing again when Pip came rushing in. He had had a frantic time for he had gone to the flat as soon after the explosion occurred as he could. The wardens would not allow him inside, and when he did get in he found the flat completely wrecked, and we were not there. He jumped, of course, to the conclusion that we had both been killed and had been taken away, until one of the porters told him that he had seen me swinging that absurd girdle and walking off singing. 'And what's more, sir, 'er 'air's gone grey,' he added.

We had breakfast in the restaurant of Chelsea Cloisters, and picking up the morning paper to read I found that the print was blurred so that I could not read a line of it. Last night it had been quite simple to read newsprint, but from now on I should never be able to read without glasses. That's war for you!

5

Pride, pomp, and circumstance of glorious war!
WILLIAM SHAKESPEARE

WE SHOULD have been in a dreadful plight if Roddy Rich, my publisher, had not come most valiantly to my rescue. I shall never cease to be grateful for that. He and his wife lived in Flat 42 on the other side of Cranmer Court and that morning were leaving for a ten days' holiday in Scotland. Hearing of our plight, Georgie Rich, his wife, came rushing to us and handed over the key of her own flat, something very few would have done. During the morning we moved across there; it was almost as if another miracle had happened.

The major worry was Rosa, who had become increasingly odd. Nowhere in the chaos could we find that confounded angel of hers, and then it transpired that she had a very special piece of string that she had prized for years, and at all costs she must retrieve it. We could not find that either. In the end we got a doctor to her, and acting on his advice took her to a convent in the Bayswater Road where she had friends, had been before, and said she could be happy.

There was nothing else that we could do.

During the day we made some attempt to clear the flat a little; the local people were kindness itself. At that time the feeling of comradeship in London was tremendous, as standing side by side we fought the common enemy. I did not know then that when the end came this would go, perhaps for ever. It was a lovely bond none of us could afford to break.

My diary reads:

April 16th, 1941

Quite the most ghastly air-raid of the war, and I thought that I should die in it. Our flat went to glory at three a.m. with a land mine. Thank God we are still here. Robbie mourns our goods and chattels, but we have each other left and that is important. The moment I could I wired my father to say I was all right lest he heard something of it.

April 18th, 1941

The remains of our furniture have been moved into Flat 42 for storage *pro tem*. Everyone has been more than kind. I have never seen such a mess as these flats are in, I do not know how many were killed, it is said only eleven. We are in Roddy Rich's flat, it is so good of them.

April 21st, 1941

We are leaving here and going down to Letchworth to an hotel there for the time being because there has been another dreadful raid and I am not as good as I was with them. In other words I'm plain awful. We are retiring in Greece. This is the worst spring of them all, but I've managed to salvage the parcel for the week of the invasion. That's something.

It was wiser to leave London for a time, there was no real need for me to stay and I had been through too much entirely alone. It was one mercy that Robbie had been with me on the final night. My doctor was living in this pleasant hotel when he could get down there and it stood on the Letchworth golf links, very peacefully. He suggested a month anyway would do me good. The train service was adequate for Robbie to go to and fro and he was very worried about leaving me to face further air raids alone.

On a dewy April evening our car drove into the grounds of the hotel with the sweet old church standing almost alongside, the daffies out, and the serene sprawling countryside beyond it. It looked then as if no foe could ever touch it. I could not understand the fact that we had dinner without the siren accompaniment, and no need to gobble it up quickly or maybe we shouldn't get another chance.

These people were living happily there, only just over thirty miles from the capital, and simply could not understand how we had been completely bombed out. 'The flat just went!' we said. They smiled with tolerant misunderstanding, then told us with pride that they had had their worries too, these had been incendiary bombs and we did not know how nasty they were. In the pretty twilight of an April evening with double summertime they escorted us across the links to show us the mark one of the incendiaries had left on two daisies and a dandelion.

'Look!' said they, with pride.

Robbie and I stood around trying to say the right thing. 'How awful!' 'Goodness! What a mess!' or something like that, and for a moment I wished they could have had something of that ruined blackened flat, of three people crouching in the linen cupboard, and of trying to make Rosa drink crême-de-menthe to get warm.

One thing was certain, they said, we were bound to win this war. I was not so sure, but I had come straight from the front-line trenches, and then maybe you do feel different about it.

*   *   *

Quite a calmly pleasant May succeeded that dreadful April, except for the terrible raid on the 10th, but what I had gone through had left its mark. The headaches were worse. I consulted specialist after specialist, driven nearly dotty by pain, and was lost in a bewildering maze of contradictory opinions, for which I paid the top price.

A rumour suddenly started that Rudolf Hess was missing from Germany. On the 10th he landed in Scotland, demanding audience with the Duke of Hamilton, whom, he said, he knew. I must say the Duke of Hamilton showed no eagerness to renew their acquaintance, and then it was all hushed up. But the fact that Hess had flown a plane over here rather looked as if there might be some sort of split in the camp. Could it be the first sign of a change? The beginning of the end?

Very little really came out, owing to the censorship which made no paper worth reading, but in Fleet Street I picked up one amazing bit of information which the reporter swore to, for he had been there: *Hess had had painted toenails!* 'Oh well,' he said airily, 'I suppose all that goes with it.'

Magazines pulling in their belts, and many of them collapsing for good, meant that mine was now a more limited field, which worried me. I saw ahead considerable difficulty for the written word, and because of this was devoting more and more time to the spoken word, and was writing plays for the B.B.C. But I had a feeling of uneasiness, of something hanging over us, of waiting and marking time.

It came, of course; that sort of intuitive warning is very seldom wrong.

I got an urgent telephone call from Pip in London. He had had a bad fall in his bath and now his doctor thought that he had fractured his skull. He was renting that top-floor flat, and although the raids had considerably diminished since I had left London they were still quite bad enough to be unpleasant. I got my own doctor to go to him with portable X-rays, and moved quickly. On his report I went off to Hitchin hospital and there booked a private room into which Pip could be moved as soon as possible. I telephoned my doctor to arrange for him to come down by ambulance, adding, 'and for goodness' sake see that he has a pretty nurse'.

I must say my life has never been simple. I never seem to get a whole week without something cropping up and I ought to be used to family crises, but I am not. I went over to Hitchin to meet the ambulance there on a hot May afternoon, and I was clasping the triumphant present I had been able to get for him, *the* orange. I had not seen a real orange for weeks and could not believe that this was true.

I waited sitting on the garden wall, and I wondered how on earth I was going to pay for all this, with narrowing markets. I must say that mine has been the most expensive little family, and I have always been the paymaster in it, till the time has come when they never so much as question how I do it. Perhaps every family has its own paymaster, and I am complaining unduly, but what with getting my damaged furniture repaired and into store, and Pip down there, this was going to be a problem.

The ambulance came very slowly round the corner and instantly I saw that Pip could not even move his head, only his eyes to look at me, and forlornly I realized that in all probability he had not even noticed how very pretty the nurse was. But he did see that they carried him into the entrance marked 'Maternity', and that made him laugh.

My doctor was consoling that night, and told me that Pip looked very ill but there was no need to worry. Time and peace were the answer, and he would get these in hospital out of

London and supposed to be outside the target area of enemy bombs. I should see a big improvement in him fairly shortly, and I did. Perhaps after all things were going to be better.

*   *   *

On May 24th there is but one line in my diary, which shows the horror with which I recorded what had happened to Robbie's last ship.

May 24th, 1941

The *Hood* sunk.

May 25th, 1941

No news of the Naval battle and we are on edge as to what is happening. I cannot get over the *Hood*, she was so mighty and everybody said that she was invulnerable. All those men dying. It seems such a tragic waste.

May 26th, 1941

The position in Crete is worrying, and no news about what is happening to the ships. We are losing Crete without a doubt, and now what they expect is a parachute invasion there.

May 27th, 1941

The *Bismarck* sunk.
This is really something, the first jolly good piece of news, and I am enchanted. I got up and did a *pas seul*. Not very elegant, but there one is. The *King George V* brought her to a halt apparently, and the *Dorsetshire* with Admiral Wake-Walker finished her off. I knew him in the *Eagle*. It is awful to be so glad that she has gone,

but whilst she was hopping about she could have done anything and to anybody. Really there is nothing wonderful about any of it. It helps no one in the long run, but war begins and then we have to go on with it.

The Letchworth hotel had been booked up for the summer months and the manageress offered us a room called 'The Harness Room' rather than send us back to London. This was really an old stable with a manger across one corner of it, and the occasional rat and mouse cropping up. We were only too grateful for the security it could afford us at nine guineas a week all-in. It was dark, of course, with peculiar windows, and looked out on to a yard on one side and the golf-links on the other. Here I did my writing. Here we slept.

Every morning the early light of dawn woke me coming in through the stable door or the little windows. I would lie there looking out on the two trees which stood on the green mound beyond the stable yard. I could hear the birds singing, there were always a lot of them at Letchworth, and I would be eerily reminded of what this dreadful hour meant to so many. They shot men—and women, too—at dawn! This haunted me, and I would weep for them, furious that there was nothing I could do to help. They would never know how deeply I felt for them, and I could not stretch out any hand to help them.

The world was beautiful with the spring, and there was the scent of narcissi growing in the grass, whilst the forget-me-nots flowered in the tiny border beneath the stable windows. I felt that I had no right to this beauty and that it only intensified the whole stark horror of torture, of concentration camp, of raped Europe. The gas-chambers were so devilish, and not one of us could lift a hand.

Yet although the sun shone the winds were cold, and by June none of us had even looked at a cotton frock. The sinking of the *Bismarck* had given me my first hope, and in London I had met Wyatt Tilby who told me he thought the war would take three more years, which was depressing again. Three more years, I thought, but how shall we ever live through them?

June 18th, 1941

We all have the feeling that we are waiting for something. War gives us this. We become aware of a secret, a plotting, something about which we cannot be told, yet at the same time get the impression that it is there. It does not need words to tell us, it is some sort of 'inner warning', if there can be such a thing.

June 19th, 1941

Turkey is with the Axis, they say, and when I was in their country I thought them such nice people. There is another story of Russia being invaded, but we have no idea of what is really true.

June 21st, 1941

There is still this awful sense of something hanging over us.

June 22nd, 1941

Hitler marched into Russia at 4 a.m. today. Now what? We all believe that he has bitten off more than he can chew and this could easily be the turning point of the war.

'Now he's been and gone and done it,' said Robbie.
'I wonder if you know?'
'One thing's quite certain, *you* don't!' and that was true.
This was the strangest war for carrying on in a series of contradictory phases. I had for almost a year lived on continual alerts and raids and bombs falling all round me, some actually on me. Never for a moment had I known if I should be dead or alive

in the next five minutes, because death happened so easily. Now down at Letchworth there was no sign of war except in the very dismal food. Nothing ever happened. It was the most lovely time of the year, with flowers everywhere and the calm which I frankly did not understand. But in the end the calm helped me.

I worked hard. The letters for *Woman's Own* were two and three hundred a day, for early in the war I had staked a claim with a chemist on certain products for my readers, so could get these when nobody else could.

I was working hard, too, for the prisoners-of-war, for this was a cause that had a very warm place in my heart. I had adopted some Australians and New Zealanders who had no people here in England and I wrote to them almost every Sunday morning. Mostly they were sheep-farmers asking me horrifying questions about sheep-farming in England. I tried to be helpful, I am sure I wasn't really, but I did convey to them a warmth and a friendship which helped a little.

One of these men was clever enough to get a code going with me. I happened to show one of his letters to Robbie, an expert in this, and I said I thought it was a rather peculiar letter and he said it was. He suggested that it might be in code; give him half an hour and he would probably break it, which he did. After that of course I could tell my prisoner-of-war friend a very great deal more about the war.

I had for the time being passed out of the panic state into the rather happy-go-lucky one where things did not happen to me. Hitler had swept all Europe before him, now mercifully for us he had turned his attentions to Russia. If he conquered Russia, then he would have everything behind him to come at us, but I didn't think he would conquer Russia.

'The bother with you,' said Robbie, 'is that you will fight all the battles yourself and accept the responsibility when really it isn't any business of yours,' and he added a pious, 'Thank God!'

He was so right.

In July my father came up for the day because he had decided that he wished to see the extent of the bombing. We met in the Strand Palace Hotel, he looking considerably older, I thought, which he said also applied to me, so in that we were equal. After lunch we got a taxi and I took him round the place. I thought that when he saw how flattened out the city was he would be horrified, but oh no! He accepted it with the calm of the very old. St. Clement Danes did not concern him; he was more perturbed for St. Bride's because he had catalogued the deeds there and so had a personal interest. He completely ignored the shambles of the publishing houses which had worried me so much, and when I said, 'But, Dad, it *is* pretty awful,' he nodded. He said that war was always awful, and that was that! England would recover in the long run, and start all over again, and then there'd be another war because there always was.

It was hardly comforting and anyway he was so right.

At the end of the ride we went back to Paddington and I put him on the train for Stratford. He was apparently getting more to eat in Warwickshire than we got in Hertfordshire, for all hotels were pulling in their belts and one had to sympathize with them, for menus were difficult to manage.

Usually our dinner was baby chicken, sparrow size, and not a mouthful on it. Often I had to go later to a friend's house and try to get a bit of bread. The Mays who lived nearby were particularly kind to me, and once Olive May gave me an egg as well, which I knew she could not afford to part with, so then I daren't ask for bread any more.

Today few people realize the horror of not being able to buy a single item without spending a coupon. Often I thought if only I could have got hold of one of those very large Bath buns the lord-in-waiting had brought out to Queen Mary waiting in the car outside Fortt's! That would indeed be something.

Now the hotel had all our coupons save those for clothes and sweets and we had no means of buying anything except a very meagre bull's-eye about once a month.

Friday, July 18th, 1941

Russia still holds on. The heat wave broke with St. Swithin, and it was over 90° in the shade. We are wondering if England is about to invade because large barges have been seen in lorries going coastwards, and many soldiers are on the move. On July 20th Colonel Britton is broadcasting a V. programme and he says there will be something coming that we can be very V. about. This V. business is all over the Continent. The Beethoven 9th symphony beats out the morse V. The Germans have been so peeved that they have tried to pretend that it is for a German victory, but as victory in German begins with an S, that is a pretty poor pretence.

For amusement there was little to be done in Letchworth. One walked, went into Hitchin in the bus, or just dawdled about the garden. But I was getting up social evenings in the hotel to contribute funds to the prisoners-of-war fund. These parties were of games rather after the nature of a children's party, to be played by grown-up people. Everyone was only too anxious to enjoy themselves; we longed to laugh and forget war if only for the time being.

One night, when we had a real old rowdy going on quite late, Ralph Lynn was staying with us—playing at the Letchworth theatre—and he heard the noise when he got in. He asked the porter what it was all about, then sent me down a pound contribution to the funds, which I thought very good of him. All he got out of it was being kept awake when he wanted to go to sleep, and I did appreciate what he did.

July 22nd, 1941

Much better weather at last and actually some hot days. Have the greatest difficulty in buying cigarettes now. The V. campaign has caught on and is going hot and strong. Everyone and everything has V.'s on it, even one of the Friesian cows in the paddock beyond my window has a great V. painted on a white patch on its backside!

July 29th, 1941

I went up to London to work and it was a difficult day, very hot and thundery, and I got very tired. Churchill has now warned us against invasion on September the first. It seems we can never get away from this horror, it goes on and on. I've had about enough of waiting for it anyway. More V. signs on cows' backsides. I wonder if it does any good and why the fat pink pigs have been left out of it.

August 1st, 1941

A long letter from Brigadier le Cornu who thinks invasion will never come. He is one of the charmingly gay people whom I adore, and is up North in charge of the A.T.S. He just wrote to me, 'Invasion be damned for a tale!' and then, 'Much worse things are happening here.' Apparently an A.T.S. corporal gave birth to a male child on the parade ground! The Brigadier's main worry was that she was in uniform at the time! Different things upset different people.

August 6th, 1941

There were five bombs on Hitchin last night and this has properly upset the locals, who think it is most unfair. We sent a whole world of planes over to Germany tonight, and I stood on the golf links for ages watching them go. The double summertime makes it so lovely about eleven at night, which is the hour when they set out. One just prays that all will return but knows they won't. I wonder if we shall ever be truly happy again after this war when we all lose so much and gain so little.

Almost every night I watched what the official communiqués called 'a powerful force' start forth. The sky seemed to be smothered with these great planes, in very definite formation, and the echo of their engines was left behind them long after they themselves had departed.

Unhappily, my health was still deteriorating, and the headaches were being almost beyond endurance. My feelings were 'get the war over, then I can attack them properly, but not now. Now there is too much to be done that is more important.'

There was a lot of rain that year. The raiders were occasionally over, and every now and then one of them came Letchworth way and you could hear the echo of a bomb being dropped. In the open country the sound travelled farther than in London and somehow or other seemed to intensify. One morning lying awake I heard one coming over and saw an explosion Hitchin way; the flash from it was blinding. The peculiar thing is that until that moment I had never realized that bombs did flash. Had I stopped to think about it, of course I should have known, and now I hardly liked to confess my ignorance, though I did tell Robbie.

'That's so exactly like you,' he said, 'what did you suppose happened when a bomb went off?'

I was hurt.

There were just the few amusements drifting into a dull everyday life. I opened the sports afternoon at a munitions factory and judged the beauty show. Before I set off from the hotel for this the porter told me that his best girl was in the competition, and he expected me to do the right thing by her, and as he put it 'act like a lady'. I did not know which one she was, thank goodness, but I had to admit that I was disappointed and could not imagine a poorer-looking lot. After much forethought I gave the prize to the girl who I thought was the best of a bad lot. When I got home a very sulky hall porter greeted me with lamentations. He thought that the prizewinner had been plain awful. Plain was the operative word. 'Who would have thought that of you, madam?'

he asked me. Pip agreed with him. He frankly could not imagine what I was thinking about. Somewhat piqued I explained that there were set measurements and good and bad points by which one abided. The winner had come nearer to the right measurements than any of the others. They still argued, and obviously I had done the wrong thing.

Beyond the window of my stable all manner of squads of the Home Guard drilled in the yard. They seemed to come from all over the county to drill here. I took little notice of them, it seemed monotonously dull, but I gathered from the language they were short of most things, for Dunkirk had left us sadly bereft. I gave nicknames to some of the majors and captains, knew them by sight, and one afternoon had a very great surprise.

It had been a hot day and the men from somewhere the other side of Hitchin were drilling, whilst I sat there typing. Each of them could have seen me had he looked, and most certainly all of them must have heard me. I got a little tired of that stout commanding officer who went on bawling out directions in a most irritating voice. He was the sort of man I should have pictured would have fought in the Boer War, but not in this one, where everything seemed to be so entirely different. Even the uniform was fantastic—to me. Then the commanding officer started talking to them, in no way dropping his voice. He was discussing the coming invasion. He gave them the password to be used, then to my horrified amazement the general meeting place, and the actual strategy which they would adopt.

I looked up in horror, and could not believe that it was true. Not only had I myself heard, but anyone staying in the hotel, or who happened to be walking in the garden, would have got it all.

The drill over and the men dismissed, he and two others came into the hotel for tea. I was in the great hall with a guest from London, and this same officer actually came to borrow our plate of cakes, which incidentally was the last we ever saw of them. We got talking. I mentioned casually that, in the stable, I had heard all that he had said.

'Ha ha,' said he, but I thought he looked rather annoyed and he walked away.

I presumed that he had pretended to give the right password, but it wasn't that one at all. He left us well alone, and anyway he had got our cakes.

I now became considerably worried.

I had been the wife of an army officer in the first World War, and I knew that it was considered anything but the right thing to disclose secrets of any kind, let alone ones of this importance. Even to wives. Could everything have changed as much? Surely not? Men's lives were at stake. The more I thought about it, the more anxious I became.

When Robbie returned that night, I asked what he thought I ought to do. He took a serious view, and said whether he had disclosed the right password or not, I must certainly report it to the Army. It sounded to me awfully like telling tales, from which I shrank, but on the other hand Robbie was right. I ought to do something about it and not just sit back.

'All right,' I said.

After much demur I wrote to the right man who sent me a charming letter. An officer would interrogate me, but he thought that he had better not come to see me, so would I meet him at Hitchin station? He gave time and date, explaining that an army van would be in the station yard and would I please make myself known to the officer there.

Robbie accompanied me at the appointed hour.

The officer was a kind man, most concerned, and what he wanted to know was exactly what I had heard. The moment I gave him the password I realized that I had not been fooled, but that it was correct, by the look of abject horror in his eyes. I told him about the military directions, and all the story of how they were going to fox the enemy. I had got the names of the places wrong, but all these were well on the other side of Hitchin and not known to me. He was appalled. He kept saying, 'Oh, I say,' and pulling at his flaxen moustache.

When we finally parted he said that I had done the right thing and must have an easy conscience. I had nothing of the kind, for I was now extremely worried about what would happen to the Home Guard officer who had eaten my cakes.

'I'm afraid these things have to be,' said the officer, 'in war there is only the one duty, and that is loyalty to your country.'

I said yes, and almost felt I ought to have sent a 'sir' flying after it.

Later I learnt that the officer who had talked too much had disappeared. A Home Guard Colonel staying in the hotel told me that it was the most extraordinary thing and he could not imagine what had happened to him.

I held my peace.

September 8th, 1941

There was a raid going on all night round here, and I and the porter went out and did a scrounge in the apple orchard. I had had very little dinner, and was very hungry and glad of the chance.

September 9th, 1941

We moved back into the hotel after months in the stable, where it was rather grim. One felt so absurd going to a bath with an umbrella up across the yard.

Now one of my prisoners-of-war wants me to send him gym shoes. He does not know that we have to give coupons for this sort of thing, and will probably think me the meanest pig not getting them for him. It's very difficult.

September 13th, 1941

News is varied, contradictory and strange. We fear that Leningrad is falling and if so the losses will be quite dreadful. The trouble about this war is that there seems no end to it and it has been going on for ever.

September 15th, 1941

A year ago we had the invasion, for we know it *did* start however much it is denied, and I cannot think why they do that. Today we went over to Ballinger where Newnes and Pearson's are still evacuated. Most of the editors were playing Bridge, they say there's nothing else to do, and they are bored stiff. It must be awful.

September 17th, 1941

A very good social evening for the prisoners-of-war fund, and somebody got a very good conjuror here who went down remarkably well. If I had not had such a rotten headache I should have enjoyed every moment of it.

Winston Churchill had forecast war ending in 1943, and we just lived for that moment for it would be the start of being able to live again. This wasn't living; it was just existing and praying that we should survive if the big showdown came.

But I was glad we had left London to come down here, for the headaches were not getting better, and now I had most horrible attacks of exhaustion, very hard to bear. I don't think I could have stood being alone at night in the flat in my present state, though I would have tried it. Maybe it was that the war was lasting too long, and the food was so bad that it did not help us.

G

6

War is death's feast.
PROVERBS

BOTH of us came to the conclusion that really I am not the person to live for long without a home behind me; its interest and stimulation help me, I need a place of my own. It was obvious that it would be many moons before we could hope to settle down in London again, although there had never been a really bad raid since we had left the capital, for soon after that Herr Hitler turned his vigorous attentions to Russia.

In the hotel food was short. This was happening everywhere, and it was not easy to make the allotted rations go the rounds. For some time now I had been doing what most Englishwomen did: I had never eaten my butter ration but had handed it over to the men without admitting it, just saying, 'This is yours,' which they seemed to believe. I did not realize that it was foolish because it lowered one's powers of resistance, I just thought it was a nice thing to do. Readers had been quite wonderful in sending me eggs, and I shall never forget how good they were, or how lost I should have been without them. There was one noble friend who sent me eggs weekly, labelled 'Pyrex, with care'. Every time I saw it I thought, 'One of these days!' but somehow that never happened. From Ireland there came boxes of eggs, and it took me weeks to discover that inside the lid flat as a piece of bread there was always butter for me. The box had to be returned and I must have sent pounds of it back because I had not got the idea, which was an awful pity.

I had always hoped that one day I should buy a home of my own, but up to this date my efforts in this direction had met with disaster in no measured way. The little bungalow I built in Frinton after the first World War, and had to sell the piano to pay the final sum required, had been a failure. I had had a house in Oxted which drove me mad. And although the thought of my own home was always the fairy doll on my life's Christmas tree, I knew deep down within me that it was just a wee bit out of reach. At Letchworth the thought came back.

There were some people in Letchworth whom I had known in 1919. The husband had been one of the R.F.C. patients in the home for wounded officers where I had been working, and he recognized me. They asked me to tea one afternoon, and as I entered their very pretty garden I thought, 'This is the sort of place all my friends get and I can never find for myself.'

The house stood on a hill and one entered the lower gate past a long pool with irises at the brim, and climbed little steps to the lawn, and the amiable verandah wreathed with roses. The house was ugly from the outside, but could later be stuccoed white and given a good reed thatch which would have made it quite enchanting. The sitting-room was pleasant, the dining-room had charm. I went all over it and was attracted to it, it was the sort of place I should have wanted for myself if only I could have had a house. Then he told me that his appointment in Letchworth was being changed, and he would be going north. He would sell the place.

The sudden thought of buying the place with the cypresses on either side of the front door, roses on the verandah, and a huge balcony opening from the main bedroom where on hot summer nights one could sleep, appealed to me.

'I suppose you wouldn't give me first refusal?' I asked.

I got it.

When Robbie returned that evening I told him what had happened, walking out across the golf links to meet him so that he would get the news bright and early. The furniture would be far safer down here than it was in store in Croydon. If the war ended house property would go up in price without a doubt, and two thousand five hundred today would possibly be five thousand then.

Robbie has always been most interested in my ideas, and can perhaps be relied upon to fall in with any one of them. He loved the garden, perhaps it was the thought of the garden that stirred us most, and we decided to make a bid for it.

The next thing to do was to get a solicitor on the job and I got hold of an old friend of my father's who lived nearby. I wrote to my father and told him what I was doing, and received a cryptic postcard back:

'Don't for heaven's sake employ him.
He's mad, and always has been.

DAD'

I admit that it had occurred to me that this very eminent solicitor was perhaps a trifle eccentric. He had originally met me by the simple method of stopping his groggy little car at the bus queue in Hitchin and asking if I'd care for a lift back to Letch-worth. Accepting this kind offer I had the most hair-raising journey back with him, for frankly he drove a car worse than I did, which was something. He admitted it valiantly, but added vaguely, 'Anyway I get through somehow.' It struck me that there might come the day when he did not get through so satisfactorily, which might be very hard on some outsider who got run into. He certainly was slightly eccentric. He was sure that he could help me with the house, would love to do it, and said blithely 'Leave everything to me.' The idiotic part was that I did, and bitterly regretted it later on.

There are in this world people born with extravagantly kind hearts who employ others because they want to help a lame dog over a stile, and give jobs to the inefficient, possibly because they know nobody else will. Then they pat their own backs because they are being kind to someone.

I am afraid this is what I did.

All sorts of people assessed the advantages and the disadvantages of my house for me. It was passed as being A.1 when it certainly was not, though I did not realize it at the time. Nobody noticed that it had been built so that every sound could be heard everywhere in it, and that it was in consequence quite the coldest house in Hertfordshire. Letchworth at any time is not situated on the Equator; it is notoriously cold and in war was a good deal colder. The electrical arrangements had been tinkered with by some ill-advised amateur, and at any moment the house was likely to catch fire. The enormous bath which had enchanted Robbie, who being very tall suffers constantly from short baths and beds, had not been partnered by an adequately sized boiler, and a mere four inches of hot water was all one could get into the thing. Having been chilled to the marrow in the wretched house, this meant that one could not even resort to a hot bath to get warm again. In fact on one dismal occasion my only hope lay in turning on the gas oven and sitting before it with my feet in it.

Arrangements continued.

All I had to do was to sign cheques and there seemed to be innumerable ones required. I left the rest to the solicitor, as seemed to be right and proper; after all my father had known him when they were young men, and possibly exaggerated when he said he was mad. Anyway, that was what I hoped.

September 27th, 1941

Believe me, it seems that after all Gernon Elms is to be mine. I am now feeling nervous of taking this on, because I am not lucky with houses, it is almost as though fate had never intended me to own one. Also it is so much easier to buy one than to be rid of it. Pip leaves for the R.A.F. again tomorrow.

By October plans were complete. I had arranged with my friends that I might do a little gardening whilst they were still there (they were moving away as soon as possible), and I got on with it. There was joy in handling earth that was actually my own, and all through that quite dreadful autumn, when the Russians were losing all along, I worked myself almost to death with that earth, and adored it. The garden as we ultimately wanted it began to take shape.

I went to London and saw Mickie Jacob, who was playing in *The Nutmeg Tree* at the time, and she gave me a little nutmeg tree for my garden which I valued tremendously. I went behind and had a long talk with her. This was at a time when the Huns were only sixty-five miles from Moscow. It seemed to me a very strange thing that in this war the hand of God always seemed to be against us. Barring Dunkirk it certainly appeared to be that way.

Now my plans were all made to move out of the hotel into the house, when one afternoon horror broke in on me. Letchworth was a 'closed town', it seemed, though I had not known it; and apparently it was not allowed to import domestic help from outside, and all resident domestic helps were working in the local factories. I received information brought to me by my solicitor, who was in a worry over it, that I could not hope for a permit to keep a housekeeper. We should have to do without.

It had been snowing all the afternoon and some of that coldness had come which could make Letchworth quite ghastly. Also, the news suggested that Russia would fall that autumn and undoubtedly England would be invaded in the spring. It was always the same old story. One had come to the conclusion that one could never hope for a spring in peace again, and we were all on edge.

The solicitor was waiting for me in the great hall of the hotel, which smelt of wood smoke, then one of my worst allergies. I asked if he would like some tea, he said he would and then started to break the gloomy piece of news.

I asked what I should do. I could not possibly do all the housework myself *and* my own work as well, surely he realized this? He said he did and murmured it was sad that he had forgotten *pro tem.* the fact that this permit would have to be applied for. I agreed that it was very sad indeed. It had been his duty to warn me. He looked most crestfallen, then chirped up with the thought that a committee was sitting on the following Thursday, and then perhaps he could persuade them to change their minds and give me a permit. He'd see what he could do.

I was not much cheered for we were moving into Gernon Elms on the Thursday, and to move in in the morning and be refused the permit that evening would be just about the sort of luck I got. I was not a lady of leisure leading a lazy life. I was working hard, harder than most of the people I knew, and surely this could be conveyed to the committee? Rather miserably he again said that he would see what he could do.

I was quite desperate. It was of course this wretched war that had brought this condition to the place, something that I had never heard of before and did not understand then. I said that if I was refused I could not move into the house, had I better cancel the arrangement *pro tem*? No, said he hurriedly, I must carry on. He *would* do something, most certainly he *would* do something, and in the end he went off into the snow and that groggy little car backfired him up the drive spurting blue smoke all over the place.

Next day I went to the Foyle luncheon and it was an occasion worth recording.

October 30th, 1941

The Foyle Lunch was on 'Things to come', and what the stars foretell. Nearly all the star-gazers from the big newspapers were there. Mr. Naylor said that the war would end in 1943. It would end first in the east, and there would be a big sea battle. Mussolini would be assassinated in six months' time. Another big European ally was coming in shortly. He said that the Axis would stay together till the end, and U.S.A. would be at war in the Pacific within three weeks. Mr. Lyndoe never turned up, which was disappointing, for he was the one on whom I had put my money. He had predicted the Hun invasion of Russia on the actual Sunday that it came, and this forecast was given in full in the Sunday edition with the stop press news of the invasion. I certainly gave him full marks for that.

October 31st, 1941

We had an All Hallows' E'en party for my prisoners-of-war fund. There was a bitter north-easterly wind blowing, and oh so cold.

I am in a panic waiting for Thursday to find what is going to happen over the permit for my housekeeper, for if I can't get her I shall be wholly stuck, and what then?

I sent my father a postcard: 'You're quite right, he *is* mad.'

November 5th, 1941

A.P. has come down from London to help me move in, which is jolly good of her, and that *is* something.

A.P. as we called her affectionately had been a merry little morning char who had first come into my employ when I had a cheap flat in Battersea, opposite the Duke of Cambridge. She always alluded to us as 'Mrs. Robinson and Sir'. At all costs Sir had to be spoilt. 'We must,' said A.P., when told what was happening, 'get that move done by the time Sir gets back. If we don't, Sir will want to know why.'

It did not matter that I might want to know why, I was of no importance. But Sir was the man! Everything must be neat as a new pin when Sir got back. As to the housekeeper business, that would settle itself and be all right, she was sure.

It so happened that she was correct.

On the morning of November 6th the vans bowled up the lane and the furniture arrived out of store from Croydon to present itself at the gate of the new home. Once I had thought that I should never see it again, and I welcomed it. But what I had overlooked was that it had gone into storage well and truly bruised from bombing and that direct hit. Much of it now needed repair, and repair in wartime was impossible.

Very soon another problem presented itself. The problem was the amazing ability of the inanimate object to argue. That house and my furniture just loathed each other.

This was something that I had never thought of, and it became only too clear.

I was used to moving into flats, now we were moving into a home where nobody had thought to lay a set path to the back door. Without this precautionary measure, every time the men came inside they brought with them half the Hertfordshire clay available. I could have kicked myself for not having noticed this ghastly discrepancy, and how the previous owners had lived here I could not imagine. A.P. was shocked. She thought that Sir would not approve. 'Oh, bother Sir,' said I, 'let's do something about it right now.'

We rushed madly through the work in a desperate but un-happily doomed effort to get everything ready for Sir's return, and when he came Sir was not pleased. Used to my cut-to-order moves, with flowers arranged and congratulatory friends to tea the same day, when Sir saw the muddle we were in he nearly had a fit. 'You haven't got very far, have you?' he asked. Indeed, we hadn't.

After that everything went wrong.

The partial central heating which the previous owners had assured me was so excellent was not simply partial. It was, I should have said, not there at all. The boiler was a sorry mess, it needed a complete clean-out, or a new one, and these were unprocurable because of the war. Not a single electric fire worked, and the lights fused at least three times an evening. The horror was that none of these little trials could be put right. In wartime one is so limited. There was far too much to do, and the war had gone on too long for us to be able to get up a lot of enthusiasm. We accepted everything.

We moved in finally on the Monday, when A.P. returned to London, otherwise she would not have been able to pick up her joint, a very important item in wartime, and the butcher had arranged to keep it for her over the week-end, but not longer. The man and wife with child whom I had engaged arrived and seemed to think as little of the house as I did. They warmed very slightly but otherwise were stonily silent.

The next entries in my diary show how I felt.

November 13th, 1941

I went up to London to work, quite glad to leave the place, for the house is going so badly. Oh, how I regret buying it! Already I'd give all I've got to be back living in the hotel again, even if the garden is a joy. There is so much in the place that is dreadful.

November 14th, 1941

The house seems to be a little better today, but when I have done work it is so dull. I am alone here all day, trying to avoid any contact with the man and his wife, the child is the only friendly one of them all. She came and helped me garden and planted a hen's feather because she thought it would grow eggs. This isn't life at all, it is stagnation. The *Ark Royal* has been sunk east of Gib. where I last saw her. It hurts me dreadfully to hear of the ships going down. Ships I knew.

November 16th, 1941

The house improves but slowly and is horribly cold. I don't think that mighty bath will ever work properly. It's a pig. Hamilton came over to tea with me. He says given time it will be all right, but I am afraid I shall never like it now.

Hamilton and I had been engaged for the space of a few weeks when I was a flirtatious seventeen. I have been born with an infinite capacity for keeping on with the old love and the new at one and the same time and finding no difficulty in this whatso-ever. Robbie has never been jealous. That may seem surprising but perhaps he knows he is on a safe wicket.

Hamilton stayed to tea and convinced me that the solution was the right housekeeper (he thought nothing of what was with me at this time, but then he did not know the terrible difficulty of employing anybody at all in wartime).

It was just then that Robbie had a brilliant idea.

Pip had been billeted in flats in St. John's Wood and now had been moved down to Stratford-on-Avon where his grandfather was, by a strange freak of fate. There was a squadron dance and he wanted me to go down to it. Robbie thought I ought to get away, even it if meant the risk of one of my most shattering headaches when entirely alone in an hotel. He thought it would do me good to be with Pip and my father and I should enjoy the dance. Stratford was a place where I had been only in peace, it had sweet associations for me, he thought I should go.

So I went.

I started for Stratford in a complete rage. Someone—I had no idea who—had annexed my special food parcel which was never to be touched till we reached the week of invasion; now it had gone. That handsome tin of tongue, the bag of flour with which to make bread, tins of cheese and butter and sugar, and the iron rations on which my family was to live when the enemy landed, as Lord Beaverbrook insisted they should. This, I felt, was the final straw. With food so closely rationed I could never hope to get another really nice invasion parcel ready, though immediately I knew the bitter truth I set aside a greengage jelly (deeply treasured) against that hour. A greengage jelly might sound inadequate, but it happened to be all I had.

I got to Stratford on the very day that we started an offensive in Libya, and the idea of our being able to put up an offensive at all was a boost to the morale and made me grateful.

*   *   *

Perhaps that visit home was one of the most happy of my whole life, for everyone was so nice. I stayed at the William and Mary Hotel, which I had remembered as Mrs. Cameron-Stewart's High School for Girls, together with my own agony of insistent apprehension that one awful day I might be left there as a boarder.

The hall porter who brought up coal for my fire told me that he had known me when he was a boots at the Red Horse Hotel. Once he had ridden me on the back of an old cab-horse in the yard. We talked of the happier times, for I am sure that people were kinder then, and we warmed to each other. I had noticed as I came that all the blinds were drawn in Mason Croft where the late Marie Corelli had lived. He said it had been left to Bertha Vyver, her lifelong friend, and only the night before Miss Vyver had died. I was sorry. When I was a child Miss Vyver had been kind to me. Marie Corelli had always badgered her about, and she had run the house, guarded the authoress against the people she disliked, fought many an ignoble row for her, and with scant praise, I am sure. Little fat Miss Corelli had been a dominating personality, and I should not have said that amiable Miss Vyver had got much fun out of her life. The last part of the time it had been that of a hermit, he told me.

I went to see my father and Jo, both of whom seemed much better and complained of nothing, which was good of them for times were hard for all of us. Next day I went to the Birthplace and had a long talk with my father in his office there. He was doing a grand piece of work for the Trustees. It was comforting talking there with the peace of the Birthplace about us and the serene beauty of Shakespeare's own garden just beyond the windows.

My father was understanding about domestic difficulties at Letchworth, but he said that houses had a way of righting themselves, which I hoped was true. He was not war-sad, for he had never been as depressed as I had been, nor had he loathed war as much as I did. All my life I have hated it, and as a very small child got into a row on Mafeking Night because I refused to blow kisses to the flag, protesting that I thought it all just horrid!

I could not think how my father bore up in the grand way in which he did, but he told me that the virtue of age is always that it is quieter than earlier life. He had learnt not to worry, whereas as a young man he had been even worse than I am.

His work enthralled him; he had saved many valuable deeds from the salvage scheme which sent him red with rage. He was very fond of Mr. Wellstood who was in charge, and enjoyed being there. I think by this time he had realized that he could not possibly have stayed on to endure the ghastliness of the bombardment of London.

Pip and I dined at the William and Mary and then went on to the dance. Pip had done nothing to prepare his friends for me, just casually saying that his mother would be coming down, and they had expected some sprightly old lady. Pip looks old for his years, I did not at that time. They looked at me and came to the conclusion that he had got some girl down there and was fobbing her off as being his mother when the relationship was of quite another kind. I suppose this was really a great compliment, but it was also annoying, for one of the officers kept giving me looks which I felt were entirely unwarranted.

Next day at a tea-party the young men tried to pump me. It seemed curious to me that they should want to know where Pip had been born, and it was nothing to do with them. Then after a bit I rumbled what it all was. They did not believe that I was his mother. After that it was too easy to give them details of myself which left them fogged and bewildered, so that they went back to their billets all dizzy.

My father was very popular with the young R.A.F. cadets, for he coached them for their exams. He had thought this out privately, having one of those genius brains that can adapt themselves to all conditions and to all tests. He was, they said, the most enormous help to them. I wish I had been born with one half of my father's brilliance, but possibly his greatest charm was the fact that he understood youth so well, and this in his eighties.

I went home again, and I felt better for it.

December 5th, 1941

I missed the Paternosters because I had made a most ghastly mistake in the date, which was awful of me, and I am so sorry. There was a dance tonight at Letchworth and I left Robbie with violent 'flu, because I had to go there and appeal for funds for the P.o.W.s, and we sent the hat round for them. It is of course such a very very great cause.

December 7th, 1941

Tonight at nine, over the wireless, we learnt that the Japanese went for Hawaii and the Philippines whilst still negotiating. They ave done something awful to the Yank Fleet at Pearl Harbour. Half of them had gone ashore to tea, nobody seems to have been on duty in the right place at the right moment, and as Robbie said somebody has been caught with their trousers down. It may bring them into the war.

December 8th, 1941

The Yanks have plunged bang into the war; hook, line and sinker. This is the first time that I have felt a big thrill, to such an extent that when I got the news dressing I leapt on to the bed and turned a couple of somersaults! I felt like the '14–'18 war again, when we sang 'The Yanks are Coming'. This is joyful news, because we have *got* to win this war somehow. I went to my private store and opened a fat tin of fruit salad, rare and divine these days, a swop for tea six months ago, and I guzzled the lot. This is the day. The Yanks are coming.

This was the first big news that had had real joy behind it. It was a shocking thing that the Japs could have caught America so badly, but marvellous the quickness of the answer. We were told that Japanese pilots did not mind dying; they flew right in *to* die. It did something for them in the hereafter. One would have thought this attitude impossible in civilized times, or was the truth of the matter just that these were not civilized times?

That maybe was the answer.

7

Wild war, who breaks the converse of the wise.
TENNYSON

IF ONLY I had stopped to think about it I should have known
that it never pays to be glad too soon. We came up to London
together to celebrate my birthday, Robbie and I, and I must say
that that particular day made me more miserable than most.

December 11th, 1941

Robbie and I got up to London to have some small celebration,
and had got out of the Tube at Knightsbridge to go to Harrod's,
when we saw posters in the street. H.M.S. *Repulse* and H.M.S.

Prince of Wales were down. Lost. That was a shattering blow. I kept thinking of the dreadful loss of life, and the chaos in the ships as they went, and the appalling sacrifice. We went very quiet.

Naomi Jacob lunched with us; she had been speaking at some W.R.N.S. 'do' the previous night, and had come home with senior officers. As they drove through the park one woman said, 'Let's sing.' A little irritated Naomi Jacob asked, 'What shall we sing?' and the senior officer said, 'Sea shanties, of course.' Mickie thought it was awful.

Nothing could make us forget the ships. What does one do in the face of such a loss?

December 17h, 1941

This has been a really dreadful day and everybody is horribly nervous about Hongkong. Robbie having been stationed there for four years and loving it, takes the thought of it being invaded very badly. I am appalled. To be invaded by the Germans is bad enough but by the Japs unendurable. If Russia is doing better, and the Philippines holding, this world war is offering far too many other serious problems. The thought of the indignities white people are suffering is so ghastly. Men killed before their wives and children. Made to march exhausting miles, often stripped naked to do it. But what is the answer?

This wretched house of mine is killing me. I cannot even get it warm, something to do with the actual building of it, they say. It destroys every creative faculty in me.

December 21st, 1941

Penang has gone and I am sure that Hongkong cannot hold on for long. My head has been dreadful today and I can't think why

H

it has not killed me long ago. Is there no end to the pain a woman can bear? But this is going on all over the world.

December 25th, 1941

This has been quite unlike Christmas Day, for it is mildly lovely almost like early spring. Last night I ran a lecture at the hotel, and we came home late when the staff had gone to bed, and arranged a little Christmas tree in the kitchen for them. This was not mentioned this morning so I gather it was something of a dud. Robbie had hung cigars on it for the man. At the time I suggested that explosive ones would have been an idea, but there you are, he never believes me.

December 26th, 1941

Hongkong fell whilst we were gardening yesterday. Winston Churchill broadcast from the U.S. parliament tonight, but we feel awfully disheartened about everything. What can the new year bring us?

Pip came home for a few days' leave just in time to share the family cold, for with the bad food we simply seemed to go from one cold to the next. There was no way in which we could build ourselves up, what with the snoek, the Icelandic cod, that frightful whale steak, and the river fish which we could occasionally buy and which got us exactly nowhere.

The arrangement, so Pip suggested to me, was that he would probably be sent to South Africa to 'get his wings' and would be out there about a year. Although the journey was highly dangerous, as I knew, I had to comfort myself with the realization that when he did get there he would be safe, and that would at least be something. Nobody was safe here.

In his absence it was likely that we should be invaded. I felt that we could just disappear, as so many had, and he on his return would have no clue. I had already built a brick niche under the sundial with the idea of putting a small tin in it with papers that would explain. I would put my diary there, if there was time; if there were parachutists there might not be enough time, but I would tell him had happened as near to the end as I could.

I suppose this was the sort of preparation that dozens of people were making, for the future was indefinite. Most of us believed we should die. I felt myself that if we were invaded it was probable that the city was the safest place of all; in the country we should be captured and shot, something that had haunted me all my life, and with a sickening fear. Pip thought London would be the safer bet; but whatever happened I would leave papers in the niche under the sundial.

He went back before the new year and I wrote in my diary:

December 31st, 1941

So the old year ends, and I bet it'll be one big hell of a spring. Everyone says that this year invasion is bound to come. I see no brightness in the future, even though we have the Yanks with us, and *they* are in for a nasty surprise when they find what war is really like. My head is driving me crazy. The doctor says with a sawny smile, 'Lots of people have migraine,' which is not encouraging.

In the new year Pip left in a deep snow; here is the entry in my diary:

January 25th, 1942

He has gone.

That was all!

It was so wrong that I had this imagination that could paint the picture and follow him on this journey. All my life I have tried to stem this tide, but I cannot. I see peril ahead of me, and am for ever crossing phantom bridges which never appear, but which ruin so much of today's happiness by distressing me about tomorrow. My father had always done the same thing, but he admits that now he is not so bad at it, age has helped him.

After Pip had gone I went to the B.B.C. to do a broadcast with Peter Cheyney which took a lot of time, and I was not helped by three inches of snow falling. Peter was very nice, and like myself sick to death of the war, yet he did not think that invasion would come. He thought they'd done it already and had had some ('And serve 'em damn' well right, sir!'). His advice was, 'Wait for it,' and that I felt was fair.

The weather was always against us for we were committed to some of the heaviest snow that I have ever seen in England, and were stuck in that icy little house where all the time everything was going wrong. Singapore was now being shelled, and finally I came to an appalling problem in Gernon Elms.

February 8th, 1942

The domestic help has given notice and is off. I am giving up the house. It is far too difficult to run, and has cost me too much both in money and strength, with the result that I can bear no more, and I think I shall break down. I saw Robbie coming across the links in the snow, and told him that these wretched people were leaving. I begged to give the place up. He was wonderful, but then he always is. He said that it was now the only thing to do.

The thought of getting out seemed to cheer me and my next entry was in the old style.

February 12th, 1942

Singapore is falling. Meanwhile the Hun ships—three of them, I ask you!—*Scharnhorst*, *Gneisenau* and *Prinz Eugen*, cool as cucumbers if you please, nipped through the Channel and no one so much as sent a pot shot at them as far as I can make out. The news, however, is a bit blurred. Three of them, in *our* Channel, too. I am disgusted that they got out and cocked a snook at us in passing, because that is what it was, curse the cards.

The next day I went up to London. The furniture would go back into store, and as London had been so quiet I arranged to take Flat 48 on the second floor of Cranmer Court and looking on to Sloane Avenue. There had been few raids, and nothing serious at all, so that we began to think that that particular phase of the war might be over. I managed to let Gernon Elms, so it would seem that some of my bigger troubles were thinning out a little.

All the time the snow fell.

Later in the month we came to the conclusion that we would end it sooner than originally arranged, and there was a final scene when again I ran out through the snow to Robbie crossing the golf links and with a leaden sky over Willian. He called in at the hotel and fixed up a double room there for us, and we shut the house straight away. It was a sheer joy to do it.

I was through.

March was coming in and I was returning to London for better or for worse. Nobody knew which it might be. The head-aches were worse, I was weaker, for the strain had been too long, and anyway I wanted to be back.

Then Java fell.

On March 12th the furniture removers brought my stuff out of Gernon Elms and took it back to Cranmer Court and into No. 48. As I came out of Gernon Elms for the last time I saw the snow thinning on the lawn, and coming through it those first flowers that I had planted there last November, with such hope for the future. The snowdrops and the scillas flowering together.

I thought that maybe I was going to further disaster, for war is all disasters, it would seem, but one has to take the risks it offers.

The little church looked so pretty curled into the tall trees which clustered round the hotel, and where in spring the great green woodpeckers tapped all day long and under which the daffodils grew wild. My arrangements were that if in future London got hot again, then I could come back to the hotel. Now I was going home. Perhaps I am a Londoner at heart. I have lived there too long to go back to the country for ever. Its stimulus has always inspired me. Perhaps I need its throb, its people, and its alertness.

We took toll of our precious petrol to follow the furniture van up to Cranmer Court, and on the morrow we would move into another phase.

8

The fittest place that man can die
Is where he dies for man.
    MICHAEL J. BARRY

IT WAS quite pleasant to wake in one of the Cranmer Court guest rooms on the morning when we were to move in. I got the feeling of content, for after all London *is* my home. I was inspired to be back in a dusty ruined city that had been so brave, and now we settled the furniture in, and prepared to face two other crises—the invasion of England and the Japanese invasion of Australia.

March 15th, 1942

We moved out of the guest room and into our flat which I feel is something of a real achievement. Here everything goes so easily and I like the big brown and cream lounge and the warmth of the place. I advertised for help and a curious little person applied. She was tiny, looked to be very old, and had been in good service. She seemed very willing. She is coming as evening cook. She is half my height, and I am very short, and as her name is Mrs. Henley, we have already nicknamed her the Hen.

I'm going to like my Hen. She is pure cockney and clever as all cockneys.

By my mother's birthday the snow was clearing and the weather was beautifully warm, almost like a good omen to us. I felt better, and much happier being with friends.

One evening I went to see Naomi Jacob at Kingsley House; she was short of tea and I had had six pounds sent to me at Christmas by 'Bunny' Dias in Ceylon, the greatest joy. I swapped a pound of tea with Mickie for a bottle of fish-dressing, four eggs, and a bottle of anchovy sauce. Not too bad, I felt. Unhappily as I got off the bus I dropped the bottle of anchovy sauce and was furious with myself for doing it.

The Hen said that possibly she could lay her fingers on another, 'given 'arf a mo' '. Time was to teach me that the Hen was a most valiant scrounger who could lay her hands on almost anything given 'arf a mo'. Whereas in the country I had almost starved, now I was back with shops that knew me, where I had always dealt, and that was to the good.

However, there was trouble with the butcher, for our own man had joined up. The new man had been in the R.N., with the result that Robbie would stick by him, though he fed us on cast-iron rations which none could cook or eat. Robbie would have it that he couldn't help it. I did not take it that way. Surely once in a while we were entitled to a ration that was *not* just 'any old iron'?

Then our clothing coupons were reduced from sixty-six to fifty-one, and that was a big difference.

By the end of March I had heard from Pip that he had arrived in Pretoria, so that misery of suspense was over. I was enormously relieved.

*   *   *

Palm Sunday fell on March 29th that year, and we went down to Lamorbey Park to see the Sheppards and spend the day there. It was one of those really lovely days with the daffodils coming out, the birds singing, and the lake like glass.

We sat on the grass under the bursting trees, and it was such a peaceful day. Bertie was in a good mood, but I thought that Mrs. Sheppard looked much older and was nervous about the war conditions. Perhaps it is that this sort of thing affects women more than men; of course she didn't like the raids, and Kent had had a bad time. Bertie gave us some vegetables, for which we were very grateful. Robbie, who is nothing if not ambitious, grumbled all the way home and said that Bertie ought to have given us a chicken, though really I don't see why.

It was difficult to find how the war was progressing, but early in April I met John Gordon at the Ivy; the first newspaper editor for whom I ever worked, and an inspiration. He thought air raids were off until the late summer, and after all anything might happen between then and now. But he had never thought invasion would come, and felt that every week it was further from us. 'Don't worry yourself!' was his line.

Just about that time I met Ruby M. Ayres, who like myself was returning from country life, and with her parrot Benjy. She had been in Cornwall and had come to the conclusion that she couldn't stand another moment of it. Like Naomi Jacob in many ways, Ruby had always been good value for money. She told me over lunch at the Apéritif what she would do with the Huns and the Axis, and how much more she would do with the Japs, the latter in no measured terms.

Ruby felt that those people who kept arguing that we should have goodwill and be nice to the Japs ought to be dropped by parachute over Tokyo and left to their fates. I was rather on her side about it. I left her early, for I had to cover a hairdressing exhibition for *Woman's Own*, and felt wretched, for in the evening paper there had been some most sickening details of the Japanese atrocities. The fact that the hairdressing exhibition gave us tea, and had éclairs, the first I had seen since the beginning of the war, did not help me to recover.

I was glad to be back in London, even if lots of alarming things were happening and all the news seemed to be bad. Now it was an eternity since Dunkirk when we had fondly believed that a single year must turn the corner for us, win or lose. Now we were no nearer an end.

The food was dreadful, one hardly dared open a paper, and half the night had one ear for the sirens coming out of the distance; and so the war went on. The diary kept the history of it.

April 26th, 1942

I really shall be thankful when we can get some decent bread again, for this is just sawdust put together with putty. It goes soggy if kept overnight. Perhaps in all wars bread is the first thing to go peculiar on us, for it was like this last time. Cakes are ghastly. Newspapers are one full sheet, and people share a copy because distribution is so bad. There are no people to deliver goods from the smaller shops; Harrod's deliver one day a week only, and nearly all the big shops do the same thing. The evening performances at the theatres all start at 6.30 so that we can hope to get home by blackout time.

There is a ghastly rumour now that furnishing material is about to be rationed, and I was trying to pick up some of a suitable pattern to put tails on Robbie's shirts so that I can re-cuff and re-collar with the bits I cut off. I have even got him a whole shirt out of a diaper patterned cretonne.

April 28th, 1942

There is a dreadful story going the rounds that in Singapore the newly arrived troops were put into action; and suffering from a three months' trip out, the climate, and quite the most awful dive-bombing, at which those Japanese are awfully proficient, they surrendered. Things go from bad to worse, but are treated with that miraculous complacency of the British. Luxury tax has gone up; whisky by 4/6 a bottle (if you can get it, most of you can't). I have come to the conclusion that our calm is all part of that deadly lethargy which arrives when this sort of condition has gone on too long. Girls of sixteen have to register, but nobody seems to bother if they are called up, and generally they are not. We are allowed two eggs a week on the ration, and white bread is off the market. On the whole food is easier to get in London, certainly easier than in the country, which 'took against' refugees and evacuees.

Utility clothes are in. No lace is allowed on undies, and no turn-ups on men's trousers. Pears (bad ones) are 4/- a lb, olives 7/6 and 12/6 a bottle.

It is an offence to throw away paper, which is an essential for munitions.

April 29th, 1942

To what lengths will one fall! A friend rang me up and said she knew of a small leg of mutton, and not ewe mutton either. Ewe mutton is frantic! If I went to a certain address in a certain square, rang the bell and said I came from her about some mutton, they'd give it to me. I debated over this. I had not seen a complete leg of mutton in years, and what one could do with a beautiful thing like that in the larder filled me with thrill. In the end I went round to the address. A charming young girl came to the door. I said what I had been told and she nodded, laid a finger to her lips and said 'You want number 63' and shut the door hurriedly. I went off to No. 63, and a much older woman came to the door; apparently she had been warned that I was on the way, for she said with some delight, 'Have you come for your chemise?' I said that I had, and she pushed into my arms a great fat parcel that couldn't have been anybody's chemise ever. When I got home I opened it and there was a really nice little leg of mutton, and with it half a pound of butter and some biscuits in a tin. My lucky day!

*　　　*　　　*

My father came up to London on a visit; he had waited for the good weather for this. As I had no guest room for him in Cranmer Court I got a room at the Sloane Court Hotel, because they had a very good air-raid shelter which I thought vital for an old man. When he arrived he expressed interest in the war, stoically sure that we were quite unbeatable, and completely happy that sooner or later it would all be over and that would be the day of days! I don't think it ever occurred to him that possibly he would never live to see the peace come. Perhaps age has found the secret of happy living, for it puts on blinkers. I rather hoped so. Although we lost Burma the very day that he came up, and Norwich—the capital city of his own county—had been horribly bombed and was cruelly scarred, he was quite undaunted.

He dined with us and we got him back to the hotel at eight that evening, knowing this was the dubious time of day, and sure enough at eight-thirty the siren went and a really nasty little raid began. I rang up an hour later to know if he was safe, and they told me that he had gone out to see the fun! That was so like my dad, and if he had got hurt I realized that everyone would have blamed me for letting him get himself mixed up in it, when nothing that I could have done would have stopped him.

The next morning I went round bright and early and gave him some stern-mother stuff, saying that he must never do that again.

'It's dangerous,' I told him.

'Not to me,' he replied, his blue eyes twinkling. 'I rather like a bit of fun now and again, and I can tell you that it gets pretty dull down at Stratford.'

'That's why I got you down there,' I reminded him.

'Yes, I know; anyway last night on the Embankment I had a very nice time, and saw quite a lot that I've wanted to see since the war began. I thought the police were awfully good. Wonderful chaps, aren't they?'

The one fact remained that he had enjoyed it no end, and this in spite of the fact that a short time ago he had been bombed out and, one would have thought, might have been lastingly nervous as a result.

Fortunately I got him on to the train for Stratford just before a much nastier raid began, one which made me feel quite sick; memory of the time when I was bombed, and something which I was to find did not improve with the years. It ended in a shattering headache, but with the satisfaction that Dad was safe and speeding back to Stratford, which he found 'pretty dull'.

A week later I recovered and went to a Foyle Lunch where Professor Joad made a magnificent speech which impressed me very much. He was speaking on civilization—if any—after the war. He said that there would not be any civilization unless we got a new Messiah, or a faith, and in that I believe that the Professor was right. After this wretched war was going to be the biggest problem, maybe. Straws showed already which way the wind was blowing, and Professor Joad had opened my eyes to quite a lot of things that made me think.

*   *   *

It is difficult to cope with work and a war, and when you get bad health thrown in as well it is the end. But it had to be done. I had so many commitments. I fitted in things like a Brains Trust at the Arts Theatre Club; I compèred for an hour on *Women at*

War on the B.B.C. and read stories in *Ack-Ack, Beer-Beer*. Sometimes I thought that the stories were not worth it, but I went on, for the art of writing has always been a sheer driving force and I believe is the one thing that keeps me going.

July 27th, 1942

This most disastrous war seems to be going dead against us, and the Germans are everywhere. Losing Hong Kong on Christmas Day was a bad omen. Since chocolates and sweets became rationed (this happened yesterday) the windows of the shops where last week they swore they had not got so much as a piece of toffee left, are completely crowded out. The beasts must have been hoarding the stuff for years. There was an over-vigorous air raid last night and our new guns went into action.

August 1st, 1942

I am in a dreadful muddle over the soap ration. We just don't get sufficient and have no way of making it up.

This year there has been much more fruit than last, cherries, gooseberries, and quite plentiful red and black currants. The horror is that nobody has sufficient sugar to make them into jam, and that even with a Hen in the household.

It seemed that the summer came and went fairly wretchedly in some ways, with Rommel only sixty-five miles from Alexandria, the atrocities in those shocking concentration camps, too many Jewish people dying, and even worse sins in the Japanese camps. I dared not think about it.

And the food grew less.

The one great help was our Hen, little Nellie Henley. The Hen had her private methods of running a satisfactory war, and these she had got going in a big way. She sold me all her sugar coupons, strictly against the law, and then when I got the sugar for them and saved it for jam she got at it and sold it back to me. What a woman! There was not so much as a solitary kipper in Chelsea without her knowing about it.

She never let me down when I was ill, arriving every evening of the week at six o'clock and making her grand entrance with her ''ello, 'ow's Madam?' She and Madam got on remarkably well together.

One wet summer's day I had left the offices of *Woman's Own* in Southampton Street, to turn into Henrietta Street to visit Curtis Brown's, when my rubber sole slipped on the wet pavement and I went down. I must have put out my hand to save myself, for I felt a most shattering pain in the wrist and the moment after the whole arm went numb. I wanted to faint, thought that I should, and tottered into Curtis Brown's where they were most kind to me. Recovering a little later, I managed to walk round to the Ivy in West Street, where I had people to lunch. I thought that I had sprained my wrist and John the waiter kept bringing me napkins soaked in iced water which he thought would be a help.

I had nasty fainting periods, and I felt sick, but the afternoon passed off and Robbie went on night duty at five o'clock. By that time my wrist hurt so much that I had to get the doctor round and he felt sure that it was broken. He could do nothing without an X-ray, he said (oh for the good old days before X-rays were known, when they *could* do something, and did), and we did try to get an appointment. Only the previous week I had taken my pet radiologist in my car to Charing Cross station, and in a raid too, yet this time he was just going home and would not stay another moment for me. Not he! There is no charity in this hard world, I would say. Now it would have to be the morning and I should be alone in the flat all night.

The doctor fitted me up with a splint made from an old cardboard shoe-box, and suggested that I kept the wrist under the cold-water tap as much as possible. The first sousing finished the cardboard shoe-box for good, and the wrist was now beginning to hurt considerably. I certainly did not relish a night with it alone.

However, at six o'clock in came the Hen to get the supper.

''ello, 'ow's Madam?' said the Hen, then saw that Madam was not on top of the world. She looked at the wrist. ''e's done it all wrong, 'e don't know 'ow,' said the Hen, 'I'll do it better.'

The curious thing was that she inspired me with confidence. She whipped off that silly cardboard shoe-box and broke up a wooden box, strapping two straight pieces of it either side of my wrist so that I could not bend it.

'There you are!' said the Hen in triumph. 'You've broke it, you 'ave, I did the same thing myself. It don't hurt so much once you get it bound up proper, you'll find that.'

I could not eat much of my supper for I kept turning so faint, and the Hen had not left me an hour before there was the familiar sound of the sirens and the gunfire in the distance. The Huns would have to take this opportunity to be a pest, and I might have guessed it! It was a particularly unpleasant raid. I was feeling most ill and wretched, not quite knowing what to do, but had got myself parked in the corridor with the evening paper, as knitting seemed to be out of the question, when I heard a key shuffling in the lock of my front door, and there was the Hen returned! She had come through the raid (the gallant little piece!) because she couldn't bear to think of me all alone and with a broken wrist. Nothing would make her go.

For a couple of hours, with everything coming down and Battersea and Hyde Parks sending up quite a lot of our noisiest stuff, we sat together talking. She told me all about her life and the people she had served. She spoke with appreciation of the good old days when gentlemen gave her a sovereign if she cooked a good supper. And some of the gentlemen were bad lots, I gathered. She spoke also of Boat Race Day in the early part of the century.

What does one do about courage of this kind? How can one ever repay it? Apparently the Hen had her own ideas on this score, for later in the week, when my dual break had been set and I was what Robbie called 'fixed up', she appeared with a piece of paper giving details of a pending tea for the old folks which was to be held in Chelsea. On leaving, each guest would be given a presentation parcel of groceries from the U.S.A. This was, of course, just her cup of tea, but there was one difficult rule attached to the party: the guest had to be seventy or over—and the Hen was only sixty-three.

'Well, what do you want me to do?' I asked her, though a most sickening premonition of what she did want me to do was making itself felt.

How right I was!

If I would sign the paper (she had the form ready for me), saying that I knew her to be seventy, then she suggested we could share the presentation leaving-gift between us. I explained that I was extremely sorry but I wouldn't dare to do this because I knew that she was sixty-three. She thought that was a great pity! She assured me that nobody else had a clue, and with my name people were bound to believe me and therefore would take it no further.

I had to refuse but I felt terrible about it.

My wrist was bound up in Elastoplast and perhaps because of that she forgave me for not seeing eye to eye with her about the party with the gifts from the States, for she came up with a couple of pork chops she had acquired and we had the first decent supper of a dismal week. Also with the Hen's help I made eight pounds of blackcurrant jam. I am very fond of jam and had missed it badly, which the Hen now discovered, so she went home for half an hour, visited a few of her 'ladies', and returned with another twelve pounds of sugar she had come by, which she thought might be helpful.

Perhaps the truth of the whole matter was that we were on the edge of starvation, and this was the era for swapping or for

I

'coming by' food. I must say I enjoyed that part of it, for it was possible in the 'coming-by' stage to have such great triumphs. I shall never forget the day when I got a goose's egg at the green-grocer's, and knew I could get two omelettes out of it if I was lucky. It made one good and one not so good omelette in the end.

August 16th, 1942

It has been quite a lovely week with almost hot weather after continuous cold snaps, for on the whole the year has been poor. We went down to Lamorbey, and Bertie gave me three cabbages, an enormous bag of runner beans and some pears. Robbie said if only I'd kiss him and fuss him up a bit there would be more. Goodness, how low our men sink! I do not want to kiss Bertie even if he would like it. I have never been fond of kissing anybody and Bertie isn't really my type. Besides, I have always been fond of his wife and think it might hurt her if she found out. All the way home in the train Robbie kept talking about what we might have got if only I had kissed Bertie, and what a very small price it was to pay seeing how valuable food was.
Why doesn't Robbie kiss Bertie if somebody's got to do it?

Monday, August 17th, 1942

It is still very hot and pleasant and the nice weather makes everybody feel lots better. The B.B.C. gave out that Winston Churchill has just returned from Moscow, and now we may expect something to happen. Maybe tomorrow is the day.

Wednesday, August 19th, 1942

Everybody has been exuberant today and there was the wildest excitement for our Commandos have raided Dieppe and our tanks have actually landed there. This looks like the invasion. We are actually fighting on French soil, and this is the beginning

of freeing the Continent, or so we all hope. I gather the Canucks
are doing it in the main.

Later. The shattering news has come that almost at the start the
landing was spotted, and now we have lost 93 aircraft over there.
There is a rumour that the most dreadful mistake has been made,
for this is a war of mistakes.

And this morning we were all so pleased. . . .

August 20th, 1942

What are left of our Commandos have returned, I hear. I had the
most terrible headache this morning, so could not read the paper.
I am convinced that something appalling has happened, and am
sure that our losses have been fearful.

August 22nd, 1942

I felt utterly wretched about the losses on the Dieppe raid which
could have been such a help, so I went to the Arts Theatre Club
to hear that rude Edward Cooper, but even he couldn't cheer me
up.

August 26th, 1942

The most dreadful headlines in the papers. The Duke of Kent was
killed yesterday in a plane crash. The weather was shocking, and
I just cannot understand how that plane was ever allowed to
start. They crashed on a mountain side. It is so final for that poor
young Duchess whose wedding I attended, and whom I met at
Harrod's on the war charities. Her smallest son is only a couple
of months old. The Germans are near Stalingrad. The Russians
are counter-attacking in the Moscow area, which is good. It is
muggy and damp weather in England and my wretched headaches have become ghastly again.

August 30th, 1942

My head being better we went down to Lamorbey Park and sa
in the garden. There was an alert whilst we were the other sid
of the lake.

Every time we went down there Bertie Sheppard gave u
vegetables, for he was a very generous man, and I did think tha
this was so awfully good of him. He was very kind, and as Robbi
said, I really ought to have kissed him if only for past favours
and he was quite sure that Bertie would like it enormously.

In the end he left me with Bertie—very pointedly—in th
stables at the back of the oldest part of the house, all dim anc
murky and smelling of horses and stacked parsnips and of hay.
had to kiss Bertie, the result of which was six eggs, four peaches.
eight nectarines, and about three pounds of plums. I really did
think that this was below the belt and that Robbie was the one
who should have done the kissing. But Bertie seemed frightfully
pleased about it, stood there sniggering, and then when we went
out to the car came running after us with a roast chicken in a
bottle!

'Have this,' said he, 'and come back and see us all soon.'

As we drove away I said to Robbie, 'Now that's all your
fault, and I think it was dreadful of you.'

'My fault? I like that! I think it was a darned good effort. I
knew that Bertie'd like it, and why not please the old boy if you
can, and give him a bit of a kick?'

September 3rd, 1942

This is the day of national prayer. There have been great argu-
ments about the rights and wrongs of leaving off work to pray.
I don't really know what it all amounts to.
Val Gielgud and I had lunch and left the war well out of it as we
talked plays.

★   ★   ★

My own plays were worrying me. I had written one with Mabel Constanduros and naturally wanted to see it produced. The Lord Chamberlain wished to see us about seven points in the play which he did not feel he could pass and suggested we made an appointment to see him. The moment this happened Mabel became difficult. She did not want to go to Windsor Castle to see him, and as they were all lines that she herself had written I felt that this was really her business. In the end however I decided that as someone had to go I must be the one, though where I should get the petrol for it I did not know. The Hen had nothing to do with petrol, so she could not help me.

On the 16th I went off to Windsor using my own precious petrol in the car with Robbie. At the entrance to the castle the men there taking down my name and learning why I had come expressed the greatest regret that I was alone, for they had wanted to see Mabel (Mrs. Buggins of the B.B.C.). I was wary, said I was sorry, and then drove on into a part of the castle where I had never been before. The whole place looked lovely, and a magnificent footman called Arthur (I discovered that early in our acquaintance) escorted me into a quite small, quite dull room to await my host.

The room was not private yet was not wholly an office, I felt, and I sat down on a sombre sofa, with an occasional table by my side. On it was a white cardboard box, the kind in which one buys cigarettes, only this had no printing on it, only two words in one corner; the two words were 'Baby's Bottom'. I could not imagine what this was supposed to be, or how it had got there, and it fascinated me. In the end I decided to ignore it completely and never give it another thought, though that wasn't easy.

The man I saw was charming. He seemed surprised that I was fully prepared to meet him on all his queries. In the end he passed two of the points which he had originally queried, and the other five I promised to remove. Under these conditions the play could then go ahead, he told me, and I felt that was something. We liked each other, and we parted the best of friends.

The moment I had left the castle I went to a public call box and telephoned Mabel in her flat to tell her what had happened. I privately felt that I had done well to get two points as it were on a plate, but Mabel did not take this same line of thought. She felt that I should have got away with all of them (impossible from the start), and that I had done badly. However, when I ultimately got home feeling singularly depressed, there was a letter from Baxter Somerville in Leicester telling me that he was putting on my musical version of Charles Dickens's *Christmas Carol*, and it would run for three weeks.

I was enchanted with the success.

I suppose that I could have done much more if only I had had better health at the time, but the headaches were getting more frequent. I knew that my doctors did not know the cause, and my own work and the eternal daily round and common task of trying to get sufficient food for us were in themselves too hard a drive.

October 7th, 1942

This morning there has been a shocking set-to here and the papers are up in arms. The Germans have now threatened to put prisoners from the Dieppe raid in chains, and there is a positive outcry about this.

October 8th, 1942

The Germans have carried out their threat and as a reprisal we are putting some of their prisoners in chains who are here with us. Tonight there are crowds of planes going about.

October 9th, 1942

The Germans are now threatening us that if we do put their men in chains in an equal number, their reprisal will be to fetter three times the number of ours. What a people, and what shocking ideas they have! Anyway we are going to ignore this, though it may be hard on our men, surely?

October 12th, 1942

We went to see *Flare Path*, which I found to be a most entrancing play, and we did so enjoy it. It was a cold night but very bright, and the news which came today from Stalingrad has been marvellous. The Dieppe prisoners are still manacled and all of us are feeling furious over it. Only the Huns could think of such a thing at such a time.

October 13th, 1942

I had a lot of X-rays done of my head after a really terrible headache and pain even greater than I thought anyone could bear. I cannot believe that it is possible to continue living in such horror. Now dehydrated meat is the latest shocker.

October 18th, 1942

Today I had a cable from Pip saying that he is returning.

November 1st, 1942 (All Saints)

There has been a third bad raid on Canterbury and all three took place in one lot of 24 hours. We are horrified. There is a strange story that early that first morning blood was seen on the wall of the cathedral near where Thomas à Becket was murdered. It was the red sand in the bricks, but it gave the eerie impression that the cathedral bled for its followers.

It was a passing detail that at this time my first three-act play was produced at Leicester, and I had to go up for final rehearsals and opening night. I spent hours listening to what seemed to be the worst lines that I had ever written, and the night before we opened I developed laryngitis, which was a horror seeing that within a few hours for the first time I should go forward to the footlights to answer the call of 'Author, Author'.

I was told that we had started a second front in Morocco, but was so occupied with the play that I could think of nothing beyond it—for the moment anyhow.

On the first night I sat at the back of the circle waiting for it to start and ate a complete handkerchief in my anxiety. By not speaking all day (a very considerable trial for me for I like nothing better than 'ever such a nice talk') I had conserved my voice for that awful speech. There was a downpour of rain that night, and the Royal Theatre was ancient—decrepit would be more truthful—so that I had to step over and into huge puddles as I went across the stage to the footlights. I hated finding myself there, and privately had thought the play was bad, perhaps because I had expected so much more of myself. One sets high standards, possibly those which no man can live up to, but it is maddening when one misses them.

Whilst concentrating on the play at Leicester the war news had improved. Next day I wrote:

November 10th, 1942

I returned home with the world's worst cold, and was almost speechless, but very glad to be back and have done with plays *pro tem.*

There are American landings all along the North African coast, we hear, and I can only thank God that this isn't this day last year when I moved into that fiasco house at Letchworth.

Churchill has made what I hope will be an historic statement, now we should be at the end of the beginning, and that indeed *is* something. It is the first time that he has ever said this much.

Wednesday, November 11th, 1942

I do believe that this could easily be the last Armistice Day of World War Number Two! North Africa has caved in. Churchill says that we have had a major victory and the church bells are to ring on Sunday. I so hope poor old Mrs. Horseman at Preston post office won't hear them and so be frightened. There is an almighty pea-souper, but a few flags are out, and I treated myself to a second coffee at the Golden Bud to celebrate. (Nothing like going the whole hog!)

Friday, November 13th, 1942

We have regained Bardia and Tobruk. Smuts says that we shall have a major offensive in 1943 and the war will end in 1944. This is later than I had thought, somewhat of a disappointment, but there is always the hope that he doesn't know. On second thoughts, I'm much afraid he probably does know. Today they charged me one-and-sixpence for a cauliflower! Did you ever hear of such a thing! It ought to have been threepence.

November 15th, 1942

The church bells rang in London today and that was the most beautiful sound in all the world. They were to celebrate the Libyan victory. I just could not believe that it was true. Perhaps I had forgotten how utterly lovely that sound can be, and how every Sunday when I was a child the music of the bells came across the valley to us. In those days Lower Quinton had magnificent bellringers, the best in the neighbourhood, and they played hymn tunes. On a summer's night in the Cotswolds the sound of them was quite perfect. Today, after all these years, the bells of London brought the memory back.

My father came up to London that week because he needed more clothes and I had promised to get them for him. He and I went to Lillywhite's and got some really beautiful boots for him. He suffered from the cold; it was his years, I felt. He had the coupons and I had the money and by real luck we got some fur-lined boots like those the pilots wore for flying. Dad was enchanted. He had never known that such things were made.

The bother was that at this time my head was being very bad, and it was a race as to whether I could get him back on to the home train before I collapsed, or not. I thought I had got there without his guessing that was happening, for I should have hated him to know the pain in which I lived. It is even more dreadful for those who love you, for they in their helplessness suffer even more than you do. He won't guess, I thought, he's getting very old; and I hoped that the years had smudged his keener percep-tions. He wrote that night praying me to find a new doctor, someone who could really help me, because he was sure that this was not migraine at all, a complaint that he had had for a time; he felt this was a mechanical trouble, and in this he was right. However, he did not realize the immense difficulty of finding someone who could help me. The road I felt I was treading to dusty death was too painful and too long.

I put that behind me, or tried to.

In December I dined in mess with the A.T.S. who were somewhere in the neighbourhood of the Albert Hall, and I lectured afterwards on beauty to two hundred and fifty of them. Robbie was asked but wouldn't come.

'I'd come if they were Wrens' he said. 'In the Navy we learn to cook, and you're going to find that the Army doesn't. You'll regret this one.'

I tried to be high and mighty but that night, when I was wrestling with the toughest piece of ewe mutton I have ever met, and the soggiest milk pudding—and I cannot *stick* milk puddings, even the best kind—I could only feel that Robbie had been right.

Now at this time in the war it was difficult to lecture on beauty because the opportunities to buy the products were so limited, and there was very little that was practical that one could say. Later some of the girls came to tea in my flat. I thought maybe that for those who like Ruth were 'sick for home', a fireside, the chance to wash their hair if they wished, or have a comfortable bath, and a kitchen to cook themselves hot buttered toast, might be a help. I think it was. I hope so.

Nearing Christmas the fogs came, and then my mother-in-law died, my first husband's mother. This meant that Pip was a very rich young man and I cabled to him to ask if he wanted money. Perhaps, as Robbie told me later, that was a silly thing to ask, I could have done it only because I was flustered; naturally he would want money.

I sent it out to him.

Wednesday, December 23rd, 1942

This looks like being yet another of the very extraordinary Christmases that this wretched war coughs up on us. The shops are crammed with absolutely nothing save the most desperate rubbish, and one simply does not know what to buy. Mistletoe is 5/- a pound, which seems a peculiar way to buy it. Sixpence a sprig is my price.

Of course there is not an orange to be seen, and I have raked behind and under every available counter. In eager communication with one greengrocer friend she offered me a pork pie instead of an orange! 'Anyway, that's something,' she said.

These days you get queer produce from strange shops. Someone has offered me a turkey at £7.10.0; a lot, I think, but who wants to keep Christmas on Icelandic cod? What's more I've had enough of whalemeat, for even if you cook it with onions like mad, throw it all away and then stew, it is still fishy. I think I shall take that turkey.

December 24th 1942

I've tried to make the flat look like Christmas and it is not too bad. The Hen, having done one of her periodical scrounges, came up with things for sale. Two china plates (Coalport), three pillow cases, and a tin of salmon which she had 'come by'.

My cousin Leila gave a very nice party with a lot of Polish officers there, and we played games.

Christmas Day, 1942

Darlan has been assassinated. He won't be the first either. Why someone doesn't get a knife into Hitler I just can't think.

I gave a tea party to a crowd this afternoon, and had spent hours getting the cakes which were quite vile so that I was ashamed to have offered them. Later we dined in Chelsea Cloisters restaurant and then went up to see Leila.

December 29th, 1942

Robbie had today off and it is intensely cold with a sharp wind blowing like snow. I have done little today because my head has been so frightful. It is a frightening thought that no one could live very long being so ill.

Tonight the news from Russia is better. How it shifts, first up then down!

December 31st, 1942

Lyndoe foretells that the Archbishop of Canterbury will do something surprising and that the coming of next autumn will see the war over. He has been mostly very correct all along, though I cannot believe that anyone *can* foretell and it must be just chance really. However, tonight we feel much more optimistic.

There is a rumour that the Huns have to give a whole year's coupons to get a single blanket, and then are pressed to send it to the Russian front to help their husbands, brothers and papas!

Last week I got three dust sheets to make into new shirts for Robbie whose shirts are dreadful. When I told him with glee (for the material is nice good print) he turned cold and said only a woman could do a thing like that.

I so hope the coming spring will not be as bloody as the last ones have been.

January 1st, 1943

This could be *the* year, and my goodness how I pray that it is! Too many are dying, too many suffering, and my nightmare is those shocking firing squads that go on and on.

We went to see Judy Garland in *Me an' my gal*. It has been a very scuddy day, and the most dreadful gale is blowing tonight. Poor Pip must now be on the high seas (with his cheque) coming home, which agonizes me. Not for his sea-sickness, but for the thought of subs.

Russia is advancing.

Yes, this *could* be *the* year!

STAR
FIFTH ARMY FIERCE FIGHTING

EVENING STANDARD
8th ARMY ADVANCE

9

He that makes a good war makes a good peace.
PROVERBS

WE SHOULD have learnt that this war went from phase to phase and one could never be sure of the next turn it would take—the cold war, the bombing, the withdrawal time when I had gone to Letchworth, and now my return to what I foolishly believed would be a happier London.

There were fewer raids now, it was almost unusual to hear the alert. One got optimistic, and a little optimism was such a joy, such a cocktail to life.

By January I made a note that the Press was trying to stop our too-sure optimism about hostilities ending this year, because there was a long way to go yet, and this struck me as being ominous. Was there something ahead, and if so what worse could there be short of invasion?

Were we back where we had come in?

January 10th, 1943

I wish that Pip would get home for whilst he is on the high seas it is difficult to prevent oneself from being nervous for him. German propaganda seems to be weakening, they say. Here of course the points go far less way than they did, and the clothing coupons are most difficult to come by in spite of the Hen who is a tower of strength. The other night she arrived with a big piece of parachute silk which she had come by, Heaven only knows how or where, and she thought it would make me some new pants.

Even the tea cloths, the kind on which you dry up, are costing coupons, and the flour bags which are free don't dry a thing, but some people are making them into curtains.

January 11th, 1943

If my dress coupons have to go on covering tea towels, face towels and bath towels, soon I shall be nude. There was a lovely New Year's cartoon in a paper which showed Hitler, Goebbels and Goering looking at a picture of the new year being led in by Stalin. It had the caption 'Look at the dark man he's brought to bring it in!'

January 14th, 1943

Last night I had a long talk with one of the Polish captains about his escape. These men have been wonderful. He dug his way out of the concentration camp with his two hands. Six of them escaped, but four were shot in getting away. He and his friend hid in woods, in hedges, and ultimately got to the frontier. There a priest hid them in a church, then got a guide to take them over the Hungarian border. It was very dark and raining at the time, and he and his friend were to meet this unknown guide in a little wood. They waited in the wood wet through and wretched, then heard stirring and did not know if it were the Germans or not. After a time they could bear no more, feeling that to know the worst was better than the uncertainty, so crept closer and found there were two Polish boys there also waiting to escape.

Eventually the guide came and wanted them to wait because of the rain, but they dared not wait and started climbing up. There was snow on the mountains, and then the fog came down and they had to crouch in a hole in the earth. With the morning, soaked to the skin, they crossed into Hungary.

The Hungarians had a rule that they must hand back escaping Poles, but their argument at the time was, 'If we don't see you, how can we?'

At the fall of France he was in a French merchant ship which wanted to go south, but a British destroyer coming alongside shouted 'through a trumpet', he said, but I think he meant a megaphone, 'What do you do?' By now his English had become excited and almost incomprehensible. Eventually they all got to Liverpool, though what in, or on, I don't know. Goodness, those men had courage!

January 17th, 1943

We bombed Berlin last night which means we are for it tonight. Alas we lost too much, too many did not return.

We started on Tripoli today, and at night the siren went at 8.30, and there was hardly time to get into safety before the buzzing began. Robbie being on duty I sat alone in the corridor with my knitting and a prayer. It lasted two hours, and at its worst there was the sound of a key in the door, and the Hen put her little head round it, with the familiar password, ' 'ello? 'ow's Madam?'

I am writing this now after it is over, sitting up in bed and listening to those people who took cover coming back tramping down the street. In this hour it sounds so noisy.

If the enemy returns before dawn I have my knitting ready.

Sunday, January 25th, 1943

Pip cabled that he is marooned and broke at the Cape so all my foolish anxieties have been plain silly. He won't be home for ages. I went to see his solicitor and got two hundred and fifty cabled to him which ought to ease things. But now I wonder if I was mean.

It is very cold here in Letchworth but there are all those early sweet signs of the new year everywhere, which is indeed something.

January 28th, 1943

I have actually sold the house Gernon Elms which until now was only rented. I am not sorry.

Martial law has been declared in Germany, which looks as if they were having trouble in their midst. With what appetites we pick up these small crumbs! I return to London tomorrow but have been happy here though the food is awful.

I sympathize with the vigorous young man who complained that the menu said *Sardines sur Toast* which was a lie because he got only one and could have eaten two—or three—or four; so what?

I returned home, but had a dreadfully bad cold which just wouldn't shift, so I went back to Hertfordshire again.

February 5th, 1943

Down at Letchworth where it is very cold; there are great sheets of rain driving across the golf links. Today Lady Kenilworth was

K

talking to me in the great hall, and she told me about her visit to
Berchtesgarten before the war. She and Lord Kenilworth went
there to see Hitler. She found him simple, very kind and quite
a charming man, though he expected to be curtseyed to, and she
just wouldn't.

He kept lots of dogs, was good to them and very fond of his
canaries. All the furniture in Berchtesgarten had loose covers
made of checked gingham.

He was fond of music and children, and she got the impression
that there was something 'fey' about him which later on went the
wrong way. In fact at the time she had felt that he almost had the
Messiah touch. Perhaps it could have gone either way. It seems
odd that we know little about this man really; and who is Eva
Braun? Is he married to her or not? I wonder. Is she a Rhine
maiden or not such a maiden? Who can tell?

'I can,' says Robbie, 'that's sticking out a mile!'

February 8th, 1943

There is a rime frost everywhere and it is so very pretty.

There is now a most persistent rumour that Hitler is missing, and
we are beginning to wonder if there could be something in it.
One of these days someone will catch him a prod, surely?

I have come back to London but dread the noise of the barrage
because these new guns screech so. Battersea Park is quite horrible
with them. I shall never get used to the horrors of war, and cotton
wool in the ears doesn't do a thing, thank you.

February 13th, 1943

One of the curious points of being at war is the difficulty of
writing a diary, because one's concentration suffers. It gets harder
to get down to things.

Our barrage kills me.

February 18th, 1943

There is the usual springtime panic of the raids hotting up. At four this morning there was the nastiest one we have had for some time; smack of bomb, crash of glass, shrieks, and then the old ambulance bells everywhere going to what officials call 'an incident'.

All of us have to die somewhere, somehow, but the snag with bombing is that one isn't quite so sure that one *will* die.

We bombed Berlin last night losing twenty-two of ours. The siege of Leningrad is relieved.

February 19th, 1943

We came down to Letchworth for a few days, and when we got to Potter's Bar off went the siren. The first message we got at the hotel was that there was an unexploded bomb near our London garage and we might never see our car again. They were just waiting for the damned thing to go off.

Here it is like spring, snowdrops everywhere and the gardens so bright.

On these nights when reprisal raids were probable Robbie thought it wiser for me to go into the country as I was alone every other night.

I preferred this to being alone, or with the Hen. I was always ashamed of being nervous, for as my father would have said, 'It's hardly Bloom-like.' They were a gallant people. But I doubt if my great-great-great-great-grandpapa who ran a comfortable little job as a privateer from Wells-next-the-Sea had quite as much to put up with as his great-great-great-great-grand-daughter, a woman of peace. Dad says this is self-pity. I don't think so. My great-great-great-great could amplify his powers of resistance with port, and did so judging by the merry but crimson face which grins at me in the sitting-room every day. I am a teetotaller. I do not do this for fun, I just go dizzy on it. I'm no good at it, and if you ask me this is one of the big deprivations of my life. I should have gone through air raids much better on strong drink, like some of my most astute friends, than on sipping iced water as I did.

In the country the lilacs and the thorns were already in leaf, for this certainly was the earliest spring that I had ever known. It gave one a sense of peace, a delusion, but pleasant.

Everywhere there was severe apprehension about the physical condition of Winston Churchill who was seriously ill with pneumonia. The man had faced too much, we felt. The bulletins were reserved, and in the middle of all this an awful rumour got round that he was dead, but nobody was going to be told in case the Huns found out.

Then he bobbed up again and apparently just as usual. He must have had the world's best doctors, or the most remarkable constitution, for he took no care of himself, so everybody said.

When I went home a lady friend gave me two pounds of steak. Real steak and a whole two pounds! When the Hen caught sight of it she couldn't keep her eyes off it. She never even said, ' 'ow's Madam?' However, she came to the conclusion that if my friend could, so could she, and went off to see what she could do, mumbling to herself.

The Hen was a remarkable woman, for she came back much later with a pair of mingy cutlets which she had dug up from somewhere. A morning later when Robbie returned from early relief after a bad raid, and was worried for me, he saw the Hen and said in anxiety, 'Is Madam all right?'

'Madam's all right,' and the Hen's eyes twinkled for she had a prodigious imagination, 'I last saw her going off with one of them good-looking American soldiers, so you bet Madam's all right!'

February 27th, 1943

Whilst we were having our breakfast a telegram came and told us that Pip had arrived in Glasgow last night. What peculiar places these boys get to in war, but God is being very good and how thankful I am that he is safely back again.

It is colder but the sunshine is quite lovely, for this has been one of those sweet Februarys with April in its eyes, and that is always wonderful.

March 2nd, 1943

Pip got down at 7.45 a.m. and seemed fit, well and strong, but in some ways changed; ways that I could not fathom.

We bombed Berlin last night, so tonight all three of us came down to Letchworth for a rest. It is so very peaceful down here, you would hardly think that there is a war on, and what a joy it is to have Pip home in a world where all the spring flowers are coming out and the birds beginning to sing. At one time I half thought that he and I would never meet again. One of my prisoners-of-war has made a bid for safety. I am deeply worried that he will not get away with it.

March 3rd, 1943

Flares were dropped early all over London last night, and soon after that in came the bombers and London caught it. I down at Letchworth worried how the Hen was managing, for she usually sits in the cellar with the dog Rex, her husband and a bottle of brown ale which I supply and which I understand is an infinite help.

These raids are really worse again and I am lucky to have this hotel at Letchworth to which I can slip down if I feel worried.

I had to return afterwards, of course, but on the whole one might have said that the war was carrying on much better than in previous years, though it had the power to make me feel utterly wretched. The beastliness of war stretches too far, and whoever wins it is always too much.

On the 8th I was down at Lamorbey again on a mild spring-time day, walking by the lake with Bertie, who seemed to be convinced that the war would end this year. This appeared to be the sole topic of conversation, and after a while one got weary of listening to other people's predictions; the good were always wrong, and the alarming ones invariably came true.

Bertie was hanging about waiting to be kissed, and I was worried. I think this was a very unfair arrangement, and how it ever started I cannot imagine. Robbie, I suppose. Perhaps it was little to give to Bertie, who was a kind old man and had always been very good to us, and there was no reason why I shouldn't kiss him, save that I am not the kissing sort and never have been.

My father came up soon after for the night, and every time I saw him now he seemed to have grown so much older. Age moves very fast when it approaches the end of the road. I took him to see everything that he wanted to see, but was aware that he found the noise and bustle of London rather tedious. More so than before, anyway. He grew more tired than recently, privately I think he knew that it was all too much for him, but, being my father, wasn't going to say so.

On a bleak springtime day with fitful sunshine (but, thank God, no alerts, for I was more afraid for my father than for myself) I saw him off at Paddington. I was quite grateful to see him safely into the train and we said goodbye, my own head aching badly. If he had stayed much longer I could not have kept from him the truth that I was in desperate pain. Perhaps both of us were hiding something from each other, I my pain and he his tired old age. But we had the determination to keep up the pretence even if there were moments when it grew a little threadbare.

He and I were made that way; though perhaps mother was really the bravest of the three of us, for her courage was un-believable.

As the guard blew his whistle, and the train started to shuffle out of the great station with the broken glass roof, I had a significant feeling. I knew that we should never see each other again, and stood there watching the train going, unable to stay it, and appalled at the uncertainty of life and the ultimate decision of death. A door shuts in one's face, it is all so cruelly final, and there is no more.

I saw him leaning out of the open window, his silver hair like thistledown blowing in a quickening wind. I waved. Then the train had gone and I was alone.

The alert came jangling through the grape bloom of the early twilight. But he is safe, I thought.

The evening papers were reporting that Herr Hitler had missed yet another speech and commenting on his disappearance. It almost looked as if something strange was happening out there in Germany, and we had been looking for this crack in the armour, hoping for it for a long time. Could it be true that Hitler was dead? I thought it highly probable that it could be kept from the public for some considerable time, for report had it that he employed innumerable 'doubles', who could clock in for him, and the pretence might go on for ages.

If he died . . . ?

'But he won't,' said Robbie, 'hasn't it dawned on you that sort of chap never does?'

*   *   *

Pip was recalled to Blackpool of all ridiculous places, whilst the rumours still went the rounds about Herr Hitler. Things were happening. I went back to Letchworth in mid-March for a short rest, and the weather was so good that on St. Patrick's Day we were all having tea on the lawns under the big elms as though it were high summer.

I had had a trying journey down for railways were showing the difficulty of war and getting very indifferent. Being short of cups and saucers, which could not be replaced for the shops had run out of this sort of thing, they had notices everywhere and in all refreshment rooms asking, *Please Bring Your Own.*

In fact the world was changing. We had become a country of slogans: *Coughs and sneezes spread diseases. Is your Journey really necessary? Be like Dad—keep Mum.*

Even more irritating among the changes was the sudden ruling that flowers would no longer be permitted to be despatched by post, or taken on the railway. England rose in a vigorous rebellion over this. Apparently I had not been the only person who had felt the consoling sweetness of flowers, and to deny us these was to rob us of something in the way of stimulation that we could not afford to forgo. People were very angry.

I took flowers up by train from Letchworth and deliberately held them in my arms as I passed through the barrier, hoping that I might be stopped and so fight in their defence. The ticket collector smirked at me, but did nothing. I suppose he knew what I was up to. Many women were doing this in defiance. The hardships of war, and the gruelling horror of it, asked some small consolation and to most of us this came in the loveliness of flowers which never changed.

The headaches were worse.

On April 10th we heard that Krupp's had been bombed off the map. This coincided with my visiting a highly recommended new doctor, a woman, said to be a miracle diagnostician, but I had been warned that she had a highly unpleasant personality. That was only too true. Later in life I came to the conclusion that it is futile to try to have treatment from any doctor whom one personally dislikes. There is something in the response of the *ego* which can destroy or supplement the cure. One *must* like one's doctor.

I came home to find the Hen awaiting me with two smoked sausages, a packet of 'gran', and a Camembert cheese, which she had got from heaven alone knows where. They were mine if I could let her have some tea, she said. She had, of course, spotted the Christmas present from Ceylon and was making the most of it. As I brought the tea to her, the Hen looked at me, her head on one side.

'Hitler isn't 'arf playing us up,' she said, 'all this pretending to be missing and that. I know what I'd do with him, not 'arf! That's what he wants, and he'd get it if he come near me!'

I didn't doubt that for a moment.

The Hen had always been a violent patriot. She sold poppies on Poppy Day, flags on Lifeboat Day, but wouldn't touch any of the other charities because frankly she did not believe in them. For years she held pride of place as the poppy-seller who sold most in this area. She accomplished this by pursuing the world's oldest method, one which is bound to succeed. She started operations several days before her fellow helpers, poaching on everybody else's preserves. She always did Cranmer Court (which was incidentally outside her province because she was supposed to work South Ken. station) a week early. The result was that when the person to whom it was allotted came round at the right moment she was pushed off doorsteps by indignant tenants exclaiming: 'What, yet again? Someone came last week and we've got our poppies.' They loathed it.

Valiantly industrious in getting money for the causes in which she believed, she had other peculiar habits. She betted freely, and usually won, having studied form with her dad when as a child she helped him run a 'gents' on Epsom Downs for the race week. She had unflagging interest in the boat race, but Cambridge must win; if Oxford did they were referred to as the 'dirty dogs', 'not really gentlemen', and just 'them'. That night she never worked for us, because she invariably got too drunk as the result of a spree at the Hour Glass where she played darts with sailors on leave.

I admired the Hen tremendously. She was true to cockney pattern, and what a grand pattern it is!

'Here's your tea,' I told her.

She looked at me and grinned. 'There's another party for the old folks coming on soon. U.S.A. parcels and that.'

'No, no, not again,' I begged. 'I can't do it, you know. I shall get into quite the most awful trouble if I do, because I know that you are *not* seventy.'

'It's such a little thing to do. After all I shall be seventy one of these days, I——'

'I know, but you aren't seventy yet.'

She was disappointed in me, I could feel it as she walked to the door, then had another good idea, and stopped, turning to make a last attempt. 'Parcels with Virginia 'am, and them white peaches,' she said, 'none of that Spam muck. Proper parcels.'

*   *   *

May 2nd, 1943

Robbie and I went to the Polish anniversary of the fatal May, at the Coliseum. One of Leila's Polish friends gave us tickets for it. It was the most impressive affair, and had something about it that was appallingly tragic. The Polish Army choir sang 'Home, Sweet Home' most movingly, so that I wanted to cry. It seems utterly dreadful that any country which had done nothing should have suffered so deeply.

Afterwards we met and talked, and it seemed unbelievable that most of these men had literally crawled across the face of Europe to get to our shelter. They had believed in us. They must have been so very very brave.

News from Tunisia helped us.

May 8th, 1943

It is a glorious victory.

May 19th, 1943

The dam-busting has been terrific, but the tragedy is that every time someone has to die, and whether it is ourselves or the enemy I feel it is equally shocking. Too many hearts will be broken in war, this and there are moments when I wonder if life will ever be quite the same again.

Then suddenly my own domestic life went away from the war. On the morning of May 20th, just when we were finishing our breakfast, I received a telephone message from the little hotel at Stratford where Dad and Jo were now living.

Jo wouldn't speak on the telephone because, like a great many old ladies, she was afraid of it, so the woman I talked to was a stranger to me. My father had had a stroke and was unconscious, what did they do?

I got through at once to Dr. Murray, the old family doctor whom we had known all our lives there, and he was most kind. He said that Dad was still unconscious, and I asked for him to be moved into a private ward of the old hospital and everything that could possibly be done to be done at once. He promised this.

'You know, Ursula,' he said, 'you mustn't want him to live. He could, but that would mean being a hopeless invalid and you and I know that he would hate that. We don't want him to suffer this way.'

'No, no, of course not. Shall I come straight down?' I asked.

'If you must, yes, but it will do no good; it won't help him and will upset you dreadfully.'

I broke down then.

Robbie arranged for Pip to go for me, and he took me that day to Letchworth which he thought would be better for me. I was wretched. They told me that my father was slowly sinking, knew nobody, and would never know anybody again, and there was just nothing that I could do. On the night of May 22nd I lay awake and in the calm cold beauty of night I thought of my father, the power that had brought me into this world.

At six that morning when it was getting light I crept down into the telephone box off the great hall at Letchworth, eerie with dawn, and I phoned the hospital. My father was still alive but weaker. It seemed cruel that he should live on like this, though he was unconscious. Pip came back that day and he said that his grandfather had not recognized him. An hour later he died.

I felt this much more than I had ever thought I should. Death is so hateful. I can see no point in the planning of life, it is a bad blueprint, though perhaps I should not say so. I rebel against the fact that life is so pointless—and it is—death even more so.

*   *   *

May 30th, 1943

When Pip left for Glasgow I collapsed, and this was when we decided to give up that woman doctor. I felt terrible.

June 3rd, 1943

I miss my father more every day and never thought that I should feel so alone, which is absurd, for Robbie is with me. Thank God for Robbie, he is always so understanding.

June 6th, 1943

We went down to Lamorbey and there were overtaken by my 669th raid, but we were sitting near the trees by the lake with the swans and somehow it did not seem to be very near.
The day was hot, and my head had ached badly, it was nice to be in the country. Then Bertie came along with some eggs, and a bunch of the most beautiful rhododendrons. Robbie started on about 'it ought to have been a chicken' again. One can ask too much. . . .

June 26th, 1943

Everyone is now concentrating on the second front, and each day we wake and say, 'Is this it?'
It never is.
Today I went down to Lamorbey again and did some writing in the garden there, when Bertie came along and said he had always wanted to write a book. If I could have one penny for everyone who has said this to me I'd be the world's richest woman!
Bertie thinks there won't be a second front. Travelling back with Robbie (who after all *is* a censor and must know more) I said that I thought Bertie knew a lot about it. He gave me a very strange look, then he said: 'All women are like that. They always put their faith in the chaps who don't know, and pass the other chaps by.'
Could he be keeping something from me?
The horrible thing is that he might.

July 10th, 1943

We attacked and landed in Sicily this morning, and there is the wildest excitement everywhere. It would have to be one of those pouring wet days and I had to go down to Bushey where Newnes and Pearson's were holding their garden party and the Beauty Eds. had to be on view. It simply poured all the time, and I ruined a seven-guinea hat and was so angry.
I had a long talk with Narcisse Crowe-Wood, and she thinks that it would be quite possible for the whole war to collapse on us and peter out quite suddenly. When I told this to Robbie (in some triumph) all he said was, 'Well, I never!'

July 12th, 1943

We have taken Syracuse.

I tried to think of what Syracuse would be like today, and only hoped that nobody had damaged the Amphitheatre, or the

Temple of Dionysus which I had liked so much. I wondered if the marble pears were in fruit, they always tasted so cold, and how the Sicilians were taking all this.

I went to lunch with a publisher who made me forget Syracuse for I found to my horror that he had put me down for the Brains Trust. I tried to explain that I should be hopeless for this, but he thought I was just being nicely modest and did not believe me. Mr. Abel, the owner of the Ivy, came up and said that I should be 'vonderful', which renewed the publisher's efforts. Sydney Carroll was sitting at the next table, most amused at all this going on, so I turned appealingly to him whispering my worry and begging for help in defeating the publisher.

Sydney looked at me, and then in a loud voice so that almost everybody could hear, said, 'If your face gets any nearer to mine, something will happen to it!'

That got everybody laughing.

July 25th, 1943

Pip flew down in a Fortress and at lunch time we learnt that we have taken some of Sicily. Musso has resigned. Now isn't that something? He wasn't too slow about that one, I must admit. When I think of that fat ranting little man who amused me in the square at Venice when I was there with Robbie, I could imagine anything. He addressed the crowd from a balcony, and they had to give him a hassock to stand on to make him look more impressive.

It's fun that he has had to get out. How it must have hurt him!

July 26th, 1943

Prostrate with a violent headache again, and now there are all manner of rumours that Musso has run away with a girl friend. I believe that he has lots of them at every street corner.

There is martial law in Italy, and the betting is that a fortnight hould see them out. This has quite eclipsed the thrill of taking Sicily. It was a pity that when Hitler took them on as partners on he muck heap he had not realized that the royal maxim of the italian is, 'He that fights and runs away, lives to fight another day.'

July 30th, 1943

t is 83° in the shade and the Cabinet was called up in the night. We are all on edge to know what's up, and cannot imagine what t could be, but of course we all know they did not do it for fun. This is the war of guesswork.

July 31st, 1943

italy now wants to declare itself neutral. Did you ever!
Good old Wops!' said Robbie affectionately. 'Game to the end.'

I however seem to have faded out of the picture a little, for he next diary entry shows that I must have had a dreadful neadache and was in the miseries of depression. I wrote:

August 1st, 1943

Pray God that I die soon for I simply cannot bear any more unending pain. None of these doctors seem able to help me.

*   *   *

The success in Italy had done a lot to stimulate us, and anyway we felt that it was a mere cocktail before greater joys to come. England was gayer.

In late August I went to open a fête at Feltham, going down there in a big Daimler. Robbie was on duty, and as she was interested I took the Hen with me in charge of headache capsules.

The Hen had got herself all spruced up, she always was most tidy in appearance, and she sat in front with the chauffeur who was completely fascinated by her. As we went along she pointed out to him every pub on the route, knowing them with the intimacy of a connoisseur, and being quite open in her criticisms of those which had smaller glasses than they should, and were what she called 'fiddlers'.

I am a shy person; I don't welcome public appearances, and after the applause had died down, alone on the platform looking silly, I heard the Hen saying only too clearly in a voice which she meant to be heard: 'I work for 'er, I do. She's a lady if ever there was one, I can tell you that.'

I was not grateful for this unsolicited testimonial. But the Hen had a wonderful afternoon. She saw two little children in shabby clothes peering in at the gate with longing eyes, and herself paid their entrance fees. One could only be proud of the Hen in many ways, though humiliated in others. She had of course bought great bargains, and laid into the most glorious tea of her life, getting it twice over owing to some foolish woman whose arithmetic was questionable. Trust the Hen! I never knew how she came by five brown eggs which she was carrying about with her in the 'titfer' she never wore. As we drove away she carried my bouquet, thinking it was too heavy for me, and she sat back in the Daimler like a queen, happy as the day was long.

August 24th, 1943

We had a huge raid on Berlin, but we lost 58 of our own. Is it getting us anywhere? I wonder. And why can't we end the war before more people have to die for it?

August 26th, 1943

The Berlin raid must have been too dreadful; now there are reports of their morale breaking, but really this is a world of rumours and one cannot believe any of them. Everybody seems to think that one year will see the whole thing over, but the last year is always the longest.

September 1st, 1943

Berlin was bombed again last night, and heavily, they must be living through hell out there. The Ruskies are almost at Smolensk and when they take it I shall send a congratulatory telegram to Phyllis Mannin's cat who is called Smolensk. 'Allow me to congratulate you on the freedom of your city.' In Quebec Winston Churchill made the worst speech of his life, none of us can think what was the matter with him, and we are oh, so disappointed.

September 2nd, 1943

Something must have gone very wrong in Quebec with Winston Churchill's speech, and he is staying out there *pro tem*. We feel that Italy isn't the second front, but that there is going to be one in Northern France when the hour comes.

I feel that Mr. Naylor must have been wrong when he predicted that the war would end this autumn. Some think it may last another two years; others for ever. . . . Prices are soaring. Pears are 1/1 a lb. Piece lace which before the war was 5/6 is 59/6, and the beastliest cotton net is 8/6. One feels so utterly shoddy.

The dyers use such poor stuff that everything is perishing, which none of us can afford. As I write this the bombers are going overhead to Germany again, and the vibration they make is terrific. I hate to think of this wretched and continuing destruction. I know I keep saying it, but I just do hate it.

September 3rd, 1943

We landed on the Italian mainland at four this morning, and now nobody will see Musso for dust. He is not the sort of chap to run funny risks.

There are long queues of people trying to buy newspapers. Our Fortresses were bombing Paris today and as this is the day of

L

intercession thousands of people have been praying in Trafalgar Square, kneeling in the road, and the Abbey congregation reached right out into the street.

I wonder what man has done to make the world so difficult to live in.

September 11th, 1943

Sitting on the Cranmer Court lawn, Robbie having just popped into the wine shop to see if by the grace of God there was anything, the wireless gave the six o'clock news and the first announcement was 'Italy has surrendered'.

Great rejoicings. Maybe we always knew they would never take it for long. Trafalgar Square is quite gay tonight, drink appearing from all the unexpected quarters, and people singing in the streets. But we've a long way to go yet.

Would you believe it, we are sending coal out to Sicily! Food is more plentiful than it was this time last year, but goodness, what a price!

I had now started with Dr. Edgar Obermer (his father wrote *Pigeon Post* in the first World War, so he knew a little about writers), and he had been both helpful and kind. It would be a long job, he warned me.

I went to see Mickie Jacob who with the end of war with Italy was returning there, and was prepared to let me have her good housekeeper provided I would take Yonni, her black and white cat, who was quite superb. I said I would have both and did not know which I wanted more, the housekeeper to wait on me or the cat to nurse. I have a passion for cats.

The raids seemed to be increasing a little though were not as bad as they had been, and so the year moved towards its close. It had been the end of the beginning as Churchill had said.

December 5th, 1943

Conversations in Cairo between Churchill and Roosevelt go on —but it all seems to be dreadfully slow. I thought we should have gone further by now.

Eggs are impossible to get, though some foods a good deal easier. We are getting little raids, some very noisy but all spasmodic, though the general tension is the main trouble.

December 21st, 1943

I think Dr. Obermer is doing me some good. There is more to eat this Christmas, and I got a turkey, plainly 'lifted', and had to bring it home in the nude, Robbie carrying it through the streets. Churchill has had pneumonia again, and we imagine that he is in Cairo.

There is a sameness about the war news, a terrible likeness, as though there had never been anything save this austerity world, and there never will be anything worth living for again.

December 28th, 1943

Today the shops reopened, with nothing to sell. Whisky went off the market on Christmas Eve. And all the time the Yanks kept bawling 'Second Front in ninety days'; we all wish they'd shut up.

January 1st, 1944

Personally I do not believe that peace will come from a sudden burst, but slowly and towards this November.

Felt like potted death today and lunched at the Ivy. Everyone is new yearish. Robert Newton came into the actual restaurant on his bicycle which I thought a triumph even for a gentleman three seas over. When he was got off the bicycle he said he would take his trousers off, and started to do this. I did so enjoy it all.

The new year. Now what?

10

The fear of war is worse than war itself.
PROVERB

January 7th, 1944

We are now making aeroplanes that are driven by a jet of air
that is inverted. That's a nice thing to have, I must say, blowing
raspberries all over the sky!

January 9th, 1944

Perhaps the worst aspect of the war is its dullness. At this time
of year it is mid-breakfast before we can get any light or air into

the flat, which I find impossible. When black-out time comes (so early at this period) it means hours in airless rooms or plunging about the streets which is downright dangerous. Every restaurant has a queue waiting for it. Many shops have nothing to sell.

January 11th, 1944

My radio play *Train to York* was broadcast tonight, with Val Gielgud producing it, and he asked us both to dine with him, which was so nice, then to go on to the B.B.C. together. This was my first time out in the black-out for about three years; the last time had been that frightful night when the Café de Paris went up. I swore then that I'd never risk it again. But this time I had to go. All the restaurants have little red lights saying *open* or *shut*. We dined at the Moulin d'Or, with very nice chicken but a cement of a pudding, then went on to the studio. It had to be the top one, which they clear when there is a raid because the Regent's Park guns make such a noise. We came home in a Daimler at eleven, and ours was the only car in Regent Street at that time. (Is that game and set? Should be.) It was just about as quiet as the lane at Whitchurch.

January 14th, 1944

Ciano has been shot and I felt downright sorry for him. 'You *would*, of course!' said Robbie. It is a disastrous thing to be born with a sympathetic nature, for one suffers unmitigated horror for others, even one's enemies, and none of it does any good at all.

The promise of the long-delayed second front was yet again on our lips, though of course the French invasion could not hope to begin until later in the year. I had the feeling that the quiet time (for this last year had on the whole been fairly quiet) was passing and soon the war would be entering into yet another phase as it had been doing all along.

That came.

February 20th, 1944

A fierce raid started at 8.30 tonight, quite unexpectedly, and now everything around us seems to be on fire. It lasted much longer than any we have had of late, and Pip and I had been at the cinema seeing *This is the Army*.

> *This is the army, Mr. Jones,*
> *No private rooms or telephones.*

When we got out the siren went and we had to run through the heavy snow the last part of the way, getting into the flat just as the barrage began, and everything was screeching at us.

When we got into the flat we sat in the corridor, neither of us even daring to go into the kitchen to make a cup of tea, because hell's own furnace was raging outside, and the flicker of the flames of burning houses was on the windows. It was a mercy when it ended.

*   *   *

Shopping had changed considerably, and now it was quite impossible to shop satisfactorily in the front of any shop. The greengrocer would put up a huge placard NO ORANGES and hand you six at the back of the shop without a blush, dropping a few carrots over them, and that was that. There was what they called a 'Pool' delivery service, which meant that the butcher delivered for the draper too, the greengrocer for the grocer, and so on; so sometimes a trader had a very suitable hunch about what was for sale next door. When I as an old customer made enquiries about anything going, the assistant would pop a parcel into my bag. 'Something you'll like, dear,' she would say, and ask a couple of pounds for what on the face of it was a cauliflower and a brace of beets. In a side street you would open the parcel to find you had landed a chicken, some bacon for boiling, apples which were rare as manna, and a large bit of salmon.

One trial was that the banks were running out of coppers, with the result that the acquisition of change became awkward.

Unashamed city gentlemen carried their family laundry through the streets, whilst royal-looking ladies got into buses with their unwrapped goods, for nothing was allowed to be wrapped. I saw one with a lavatory brush carrying it with all the triumph of Britannia with her trident. Undoubtedly you stalked forth to shop as hunters on the track of prey. Everything had to be stalked.

The siren went, the whole place rocked, and you believed that every moment would be your last; then after a time when the all-clear came you turned into bed as if nothing had happened. One moment I took my knitting into the front line (without the advantage of a slit trench), and the next I was to bed with composure.

Everything was getting increasingly shabby. One could replace nothing, and I trembled for what was happening to the bath towels. In one exultant moment I managed to buy a dozen dirty-linen bags at 4s. 11d. each, with the idea of converting them into washing-up cloths. Flour bags were the thing, but bad driers, they were large and went a long way.

All the time the raids came and went.

On February 22nd Pip, I, and a man friend drove off to the Law Courts for the hearing of Pip's divorce suit.

I was most unhappy, and to make matters worse Robbie was low with a mild attack of pneumonia which worried me. At 2.30 in the afternoon Pip got his decree nisi, but it was one of those really horrible days and I hated every moment of it. Religiously I am anti-divorce. I am sure it is not the right solution and nothing would make me avail myself of it. If one is married by the State, yes, certainly; but to swear until death and then break it is something I could not bring myself to do.

But not much good saying that in the modern world to a young son who had found marriage unhappy.

February 24th, 1944

There was the siren and then gunfire at breakfast, and another awful raid was going strong at 9.30. All Cheyne Walk seemed to be afire, and they tell me much the same thing has happened to Wardour Street. A plane came down in flames. Everybody is feeling rather jittery, it is the time of year for that, for as the war goes on one always hopes to be through with all this and one is never through with it.

One does not get used to hostilities as once I thought was possible. How could one? The unexpected is for ever nudging the elbow, and even when fast asleep the merest distant siren, so faint that it is hardly clear, is enough to send one shooting up. One wakes on the moment.

March 1st, 1944

The most shattering of highly concentrated air raids returned to us last night, and I am sure they are dropping much bigger and nastier bombs. One of the Guinness Trust dwellings a mile away got a direct hit, and I thought we had gone with it. It killed 250 people. This really has been a ghastly blitz week, and how I have hated it, for I am more on edge than ever before, and would give everything to return to the Whitchurch meadows, for I feel I would be safe by the low hawthorn hedge at the far end of the Lake meadow, and there nothing could hurt me.

Dr. Obermer was anxious for me not to have too much of this, the tension worried him for me. At the same time I should have thought that he need not have told me that nowadays the Huns were dropping block-busters (I hadn't heard a word of this before). The thought of block-busters, and Cranmer Court, Nell Gwynn House, and Chelsea Cloisters all going to heaven in one almighty crack terrified me. The land mine had done enough to ruin Cranmer Court, with ninety-nine flats standing in complete ruins with sightless windows and decay everywhere. Though someone had made the best of a bad job and had kept hens in a wardrobe in a second-floor flat, so had his own private eggs!

This was perhaps the most tired bit of the war. It seemed so pointless. We were sick of starving on snoek and whalemeat. One lived in prayer for a full moon, sheltering under it and miserable that it lasted for only such a short period of safety, which meant that 'they' would soon be back again.

> Lighten our darkness, we beseech thee, O Lord;
> and by thy great mercy defend us from all
> perils and dangers of this night. . . .

March 14th, 1944

There was another vile raid. Robbie and I went into the corridor for it, and I kept feeling most dreadfully sick. I tried to play Patience, for actually doing something is a help, then I heard a bomb coming. It was making for us. They say that you never hear the bomb that hits you, but I wonder if that is true. It made a shocking shrieking sound, and Robbie grabbed hold of me; the next moment it crashed into the road outside, missing us by a few yards only. The earth rose and fell again under us; we heard the windows blown out and scattering the road below with glass, I thought the tinkling would never end. The furniture seemed to be running about my bedroom like some Mad Hatter's tea party, and I remember thinking, 'If they drop another one right now, then I *shall* go mad.'

The fire began. The bomb had apparently hit a gas main or

something in the street below, and up shot the flames and the eerie copperish light of them came right into the flat.

I started to shiver and was most ashamed of myself. Oh, I do wish that I had been born brave.

March 16th, 1944

Robbie and I have come down to Letchworth again. It is quietly peaceful and quite calm. The hedges are almost in full leaf, which is extraordinary for this early time of the year, but in 1940 when we had all that bombing we had the trees leaf twice, budding and leafing for a second time in the autumn. I believe there is some scientific explanation for this.

April 5th, 1944

The deadly lethargy of strained endurance is becoming even more insistent as the war goes on. We all have the feeling that the arrival of the new front will bring another phase to the war, and perhaps that will be the best possible thing. But when will it come? The new severe blitz has shaken everyone, I think, far more than the old ones when we accepted them as being preferable to invasion. Now that mood of acceptance is over. We are impatient, we are half starved, we are undermined.

The first three weeks of the second front may be quite awful, and we expect paratroops to be landed here. I'll look very funny if they come to Letchworth golf links, for although they say the Home Guard can cope with their pikes, I think it is far more likely that the paratroops will cope with the Letchworth Home Guard.

I was now living at Letchworth for many days at a time, because I could take no more, and as the housekeeper had left I should have been terribly alone in the flat. Poor darling Yonni had died, which distressed me terribly, not only for Mickie's sake but for my own. He was both a darling cat and a gentleman.

When I could I went to London to shop—shoes were my main worry, and these I simply could not get because they appeared to be unobtainable. I had found that I was entitled to fourteen extra coupons for my osteomyelitis ankle, but if there were no shoes to buy these coupons were hardly of use to me. Wherever I went there were queues round the shoe shops and not so much as a smell of a pair of shoes.

Letchworth, March 31st, 1944

We have our moments. It was my 751st alert last night, and we lost 95 bombers over Germany which makes me quite sick. During the evening, just as people were wandering off to bed with hot milk and bottles, the pantry boy attacked the manageress and there was something of a row. The porter rushed into the great hall to Robbie, saying, 'Come, sir, come! Murder's being done.' I gather Robbie was not a terrific help, but someone had the good sense to telephone the local police and a bobby arrived with a 'What's-all-this-'ere?' look, and immediately got two front teeth knocked down his throat for him.

What you might have called a lively Friday night. Personally I was quite sorry when the plain van took the boy off, for at least he had been something of a change.

April 4th, 1944

I went up to the factory area of Letchworth, which is quite a way from where the hotel is. There I visited Lewis May's factory. I wanted to see the special 24-hour pack which they are putting up for the soldiers on the second front (when that comes). It is fascinating and contains eighteen sweets, four pots of tea in tablet form, two porridge tablets, meat and potato ones and chocolate. I don't think I should fancy them myself, especially the porridge tablets.

April 5th, 1944

I came back to Cranmer Court for the night because my head was so bad that I had to see Dr. Obermer. Tonight I am alone. I feel that if I live through this one dreadful night I shall be all right, because it is always the first one in the unsafe area that seems so bad. More so when alone. Rumours of the second front are everywhere, and the planes have been going over all day.

Every day we asked ourselves, 'Is this the second front?' believing that to be the answer to all our prayers, yet tomorrow always came and nothing ever happened. I was having trouble with my osteomyelitis foot, too, because I had worn too many old shoes too long, so that they ricked the ankle. Also, I had not got a single pair which would keep out the water, and I think I never expected to possess such luxury again. That is the way one settles in to hardship.

Enormous forces had been going over all day, wherever one went one could not escape from the noise of them. On my second day in London I lunched with W. J. Makin, a very old friend of mine. He was one of the nicest journalists I have ever met, with a genius for languages which helped him on foreign reporting jobs.

We went to the Ivy, and there he told me that he had until recently been running a newspaper in Greece. He had lived in a cave and gone to press in the cave, finding it quite amusing until they got themselves invaded. That, of course, was not so funny. He was quite calm about air raids, and said he thought they were all right as long as you had got a slit trench to nip into, but he hated being here without what he considered to be a positive necessity. A slit trench was *the* thing! My snag was that I had not got a slit trench, had never had one, and very much doubted if I ever should get one.

We were undoubtedly living through the tensest part of the war, and less able to take it. At the time of Dunkirk few of us had actually realized how serious matters were, but now we knew. The hideous bombing of Germany continued, and the noise the bombers made going out over Letchworth (the U.S. were at Bassingbourne) almost every night was terrific.

We had been preparing for this for a long time now, and were conscious of the horror it would be if we failed to silence the enemy. General morale frayed. It was tormenting that the confidence we had had at Christmas now seemed to fade; what should we do if victory did not come, and if we failed again? It seemed hateful to be alive ourselves at a time when one felt so much pain for those about to die, yet could do nothing to help them, only fret.

With May tremendous convoys went through London, and we were told that the Sussex lanes were almost choked with them. Cunning people were already burying food in their gardens, for they thought that it might be a very sticky time in a week or two. Then horrifying rumours began to go the rounds. We heard of radio-controlled planes which would bomb us to Kingdom come; one was said to have foundered in Sweden and it had two magnetic mines on board, which was not so nice for the Swedes. The Germans bragged that they had got special secrets which would bring about our complete undoing. Time would show.

I was still trying to get shoes, the problem was rapidly becoming vital, but there was the greatest difficulty in even getting *into* shoe shops. One had a chair across the entrance announcing *Shop Full*. Another had a notice *No assistant will be free for fifteen minutes*. I had not the time to waste and turned away, lame and weary and very disheartened.

May 17th, 1944

There has been a most extraordinary vision. It was of a crucifix and was seen last night over the Ipswich neighbourhood. A most miraculous sight for the whole sky changed with it, and I think this is undoubtedly true for too many saw it. Some said that it was very comforting. Surely a religious vision *must* be of good omen, or what could it be? Could it mean that we were standing on the brink of success after this long long wait, and is there ahead of us something of happiness?

Thousands of barges were now waiting at Portsmouth, Shoreham was the most hush-hush place in England, they said, and no one whispered of what Shoreham had got that others hadn't. By May 26th the Home Guard were on duty at all tunnels on the railway, and there had come those empty places in Fleet Street, for suddenly the war correspondents were off about their business. Jimmy Makin had promised to send a last-minute word to me, he knew that I would disclose nothing for he and I had been on too many jobs together for him not to know that; but I had had no word from him yet so I was sure that this was not the day.

Hospitals were ordered to have beds clear and ready. Victory or disaster; whichever it might be England stood on the threshold of it, a little cold, a little sad-eyed, but ready. Still it did not come.

One night at the Ministry of Information a girl clerk with nothing to do practised on her teleprinter what she would say when the actual second front began. As she was doing it a message from the Fifth Army came over from Italy and she got mixed, so that suddenly her bogus message was flashed to the U.S.A. telling the world that the second front had started. When it was broadcast in the States they got so windy with expectation that nobody knew what to do next.

We had no idea of what to expect when it began. It could easily be that the outraged enemy would land their paratroops in pastoral England to make things more difficult at home. It could be bombers, gas even, what? This was going to be the biggest invasion in history, and if it failed we could lose the war. We prayed for it to start. Anything to get it over. My invasion parcel was prepared, I was ready.

It came nearer.

June 3rd, 1944

Now after all it hasn't been tonight as most people thought it would be. We were so sure. The weather has changed, and it is quite vile with a hard wind blowing, which could be the reason.

Sunday, June 4th, 1944

We are told that Rome is falling, and now I am almost wondering if the imminence of the second front has not been exaggerated and could boil down into a farce. The porter at the hotel is madly keen to know, for some reason or other, and has gone round offering to give ten bob to anyone who would tell him. Nobody has told him a thing. We just don't know.

June 5th, 1944

I have had a dreadful headache and was only half conscious for a couple of hours, and when I was coming to I saw the letters. There was a very short one from Jimmy Makin. It just said *I have gone*. Then I knew.
As soon as I was well enough I burnt the letter in a match flame and so got rid of it. I said nothing to Robbie. Both of us are in separate jobs; he probably knew too, but he would never tell me; I would never tell him.

June 6th, 1944

Now that I know, I have returned to London, and all last night our own planes were going over us. I think the balloons were down for they flew so very low.
Today I was at work in my writing-room with my portable switched on, and as I worked I heard the announcement made. We had landed on the Normandy Coast. Eisenhower spoke at 9.45, and the Dutch and Belgian Prime Ministers; King Haakon

too. Of course R᙮᙮bie missed the lot because he had gone out to have his hair c᙮᙮! Privately I don't think he had a clue that it could be today. In a single instant the tension eased, even though the weather changed and we had rain and high wind which were not so good for the men. Howard Marshall struck a mine and broadcast when he was soaked through, but how he didn't broadcast from Heaven only God will know. Hitler will retaliate violently on London, they say he has 1500 to 2000 bombers, and if he does it is likely that we shall look rather silly. The invasion date was, they say, fixed for forty-eight hours earlier but the weather was too bad.

June 8th, 1944

Now some of the real news is creeping out, and we are told that it was nearly a major disaster, for the sea got up and still is horrid. They had new anti-seasick pills which helped the men. Apparently everything is still going well, but we have to wait. The date for the ending of the war is now being betted on. I have five bob on October 31st.

I had thought that I should be very much better directly we had a foothold on the Continent, but instead the headaches were frantic. Dr. Obermer was very anxious to get me to sleep, for several days if possible, so that I should get something of a rest which was he thought a wise action to take. He was both helpful and kind, suggesting that we should get a nurse in to see after me, then I would have someone with me all the time. A nurse was engaged.

In the middle of this the Hen came on duty, wildly excited over the second front, and with a small Union Jack in the buttonhole of her coat. ' 'ow's Madam?' said she.

I was not happy about the treatment, for I don't like drugs and always suspect them, but on June 15th a quite nice young nurse appeared just before Robbie went off on duty. The plan was that late that night, when I went to bed at the ordinary time, a dose would be given me and soon after I should fall asleep for probably twenty-four hours, then to be given a little more.

That never happened.

The entry in the diary shows what did happen.

June 15th, 1944

This evening was rather trying for there were four unpleasant little raids, nothing much, but enough to set one on edge. I got nervous. I did not want to be lying here unconscious if this was going to be one of those busy nights to which we are too well accustomed. So Nurse thought we'd wait a bit and we sat up talking.

At eleven the alert went and then the most extraordinary thing happened. There came a noise that was quite new to us, like a rattling of a quantity of chains belonging to some ghost in fiction. Bombs began to drop, much louder ones. We thought after a while that perhaps we had some new anti-aircraft guns which we had brought into action, and these were going round the streets on cars, which accounted for the chain rattling. Then experience made us wiser.

The rattling came, suddenly stopped dead, and within a minute there was a violent explosion. The smell of it was everywhere. This went on all night, and of course we very soon abandoned the idea of my passing out into a deep sleep.

In the early morning the chattily disposed postman told us that London was being systematically bombed by pilotless bomb-carrying aircraft. It *was* something new.

These were buzz-bombs.

I rang up Robbie at the Ministry and they had been foxed for a time. But they thought these were pilotless aircraft. The morning grew quieter, then suddenly there were three alerts in an hour. These new aeroplanes are fitted with a most dreadful blast power,

M

so they say, and the radio is being affected by it. Big Ben is being given from a record for the first time!
I rang up Letchworth. They've had nothing.

June 17th, 1944

I think the Huns are now letting us have everything that they have got. There was peace from 6 a.m. until 2.30 p.m., then every siren started going, and these dagger-like shapes came scudding through the sky. Each in its turn went silent, tottered, then fell and blew up.
The major horror is that there is no point in getting down a pilotless plane whose job is to get down anyway.

Sunday, June 18th, 1944

This is quite the most awful thing of the war, for no one guessed that it was coming. Alerts go all the time, and they are no help at all, for the planes keep pace with them. When these buzz-bombs explode they throw up clouds of thick black smoke and I should imagine that they cause chaos. This morning there was a service at the Guards Chapel in Birdcage Walk, and one dropped on the chapel. There has been a ghastly loss of life, and some people from Cranmer Court were there at the time. Everyone is deeply shocked.

June 20th, 1944

In the small hours Robbie decided that we must come right away, and he brought Nurse and myself down to Letchworth by the first train. We had to travel in the guard's van, full of fish boxes. Everyone is talking of the buzz-bombs. They have not fallen farther this side of London than Edgware, so the guard told us. They fly very fast and do immense harm. The horror is that for the moment we have no return for them.

But thank God for peace. I never knew the full value of sleep and rest until today, it would seem. I slept the clock round. These pilotless planes keep coming over all the time in London, and I should have thought that at this rate all of us must ultimately be killed by them.

The *Daily Express* had this article from Gordon Young, Stockholm, on the following Friday, and this gave us some information about what we were facing:

BERLIN CALLS THEM KIVIK ROCKETS

LONDON OUTSKIRTS ARE ABLAZE

Goebbels' spokesman tonight gave a big publicity talk to neutral correspondents on the pilotless plane attacks on Britain, which he called a 'sensation greater than the invasion of Normandy'. He said the planes were called Kivik Rockets . . . that several German engineers have concentrated on the perfection of the Kivik since the first years of the war.

German radio worked up a full blast gloat over the buzz-bombs. It said that London's railway traffic is almost paralysed; the capital's southern outskirts from Kingston and Sutton to Bromley are ablaze; smoke covers Sevenoaks in Kent; a large part of Southampton's docks are burning. . . .

At 7.30 Hans Fritsche, Director of Broadcasting, made this speech: 'This is the news for which the German people have waited and worked for so long. . . . The British people stressed that a new weapon could not be regarded as a serious possibility. . . . There were even Germans who had their doubts, but their leaders have not disappointed them. They have chosen the proper moment for the exploitation of this product of German inventive genius. The awakening the British people are now experiencing will not be the last one. We remind them that we warned them.'

Very soon there was something which got Harpenden way and Luton, which showed that these wretched things wer getting nearer. They had not got our range yet, but it was menace for which there was as yet no antidote.

Our troops were nearing Cherbourg, and had taken some o the ramps from which many of these buzz-bombs were fired We were told that the unhappy prisoners-of-war had been mad to fire them, which in their early stages often meant death. Bu whilst we went ahead in the invasion of France we were cuttin at the real heart of the war, though in England itself things wer very difficult. Ahead lay what? Victory, of course, but when?

11

I hate the sound of war; I loathe the smell of death.
ANON.

Now that I had got down to Letchworth it seemed that I was likely to stay there for quite a long time. One thing was certain, I should not at this rate start that treatment which would pass me out. That was done with *pro tem*.

I got news of Jimmy Makin. Early on in the landing he had been wounded in the stomach, picked up by a German ambulance, and then the ambulance had run into an ambush and had been shot up. I had never thought of Jimmy dying, but he had died, and I was very upset. He was the old-time journalist, very courageous, very strong, a man who always gave you a smile and inspired you with some of his own courage. It was a shock to know that I should never see him again.

By Midsummer Day both Waterloo and Victoria station had been hit. Then one night a buzz-bomb came down to Letchworth. I had taken to preparing properly for night attack. War had taught me that there was nothing like getting myself ready to get out of trouble quickly before trouble got me. On the outside handle of my bedroom door I hung my gas-mask, and put my knitting into the shoes set out for cleaning, with the library book alongside. The alert came, and almost instantly that clackety-clack of a buzz-bomb coming swiftly out of the distance and aiming for us. Out I shot to a small niche of landing well away from glass; and Mr. and Mrs. George Levy, also awakened in an agonizing hurry, and Mr. and Mrs. Newman as well were all coming out at one and the same moment. The five of us just looked at one another, then the buzz-bomb cut out and the awful silence came. I hadn't even got the time to say 'It'll be all right' (though who was I to jump to that silly conclusion?) when it blew itself to glory about three miles away. When we came to Mr. Levy produced whisky, which I thought was very decent of him, for when anything of that kind fell fairly near to you it was something of a shock. He was most worried that I didn't drink (rather like Rosa with the crême-de-menthe). 'I just don't, you see,' I explained.

Whisky was hard enough to get without my drinking any of it for him. I remembered how when we were bombed out in Cranmer Court, and went along to the Minshulls' flat, everybody drank their tea for them. Next day I took along a small but gallant contribution, for I felt I should. I learnt to my horror that I was the only person who had done what I should have thought to be a duty! Even in wartime people are too casual over these details.

We got that one buzz-bomb, then it went quiet on us for a time, and we jumped to the conclusion that this must have been ust one of those things; it had come off its proper route or something. We were so wrong.

Across the water the fighting for Caen had begun; the whole landing went far too slowly, we all felt, and news was little, never daring to be really bold. Everything was hush-hush and the Army did not seem to get anywhere; already we were a tired people, a people who had too frequently been bitterly disappointed, and behind it there lurked the horror that something yet might go wrong. Nurse had gone back to London. I fought the almost daily headache alone, but now the days of war should surely be running out, for the second front *had* started.

July 2nd, 1944

Apparently there has been another surprise, and I suppose they would say they had warned us that it would come. This is another bomb which comes quite silently, you don't hear it coming, it just arrives. It is a rocket bomb. They have bases across the water and just fire these things across. I shall be staying here in Letchworth until mid-August anyway.

July 11th, 1944

My 805th raid and my head utterly awful. This raid arrived at midday bang out of the blue. I felt I simply could not wait for it, so I went out into the garden and lay down in the long grass far away from everyone and everything. It was an unbearably long alert.

Robbie too has spent practically the whole of the day dodging buzz-bombs in the office; he goes under his desk and says he is jolly smart at it now. The night is almost worse.

There is another of these rumours going round that we have got something cunning up our sleeves which could win the war. It is something to do with a short cut. It may be just a rumour, but there you are.

July 17th, 1944

Pip is to be married again at the end of August. The curious thing
is that in all this proximity to death, the anxiety, and the despera-
tion of trying to get enough to eat (and never getting it), a little
thing like Pip's second marriage seems just nothing. But I do
hope that she is really nice, and that they will be very happy. He
wants to come here on his honeymoon.

July 20th, 1944

The bombs are now worse in London, and there is a story going
the rounds that Hitler went to some meeting and somebody put
a home-made bomb into a suitcase and shoved it under the table,
then went out to the 'gents', and in another moment up she went!
Later rumours say he has not been hurt sufficiently, which is a
great pity—if any of it is true.

July 21st, 1944

At 10 a.m. this morning civil war was reported in Germany; it is
what we have been waiting for (if it is true), but of course we
don't really know what is happening. Another night of the Long
Knives, I daresay, and that is a horrifying thought.
At 9 p.m. there was a sudden alert, just as we had switched on the
news in the great hall, and a moment later an almighty crump
round Luton way. The nice man who was staying here last night
was killed outright, we are told.

July 22nd, 1944

Another truly ghastly night pouncing out of the bedroom on to
the landing into that infernal niche and listening to distant crumps.
There seemed to be quite a lot of them. We had refreshment, too,
Mr. Levy's whisky (I feel all this is very hard on poor Mr. Levy

and quite unfair), and we ate tomatoes because that was all we had and we were hungry. I wonder if I shall ever taste *petits-fours* again? Oh, what a beautiful dream!

★   ★   ★

We had not gone ahead in Normandy as fast as we had expected, I was sure, but that was not what they said. Every landing must have hitches of some kind, of course, we were saying; and although we were approaching Florence in Italy the thought of being held up for a time in France was unpleasant as the summer does not last for ever. And summer *is* necessary to a campaign of this kind.

Robbie had a friend called Jacko who had worked for some time with them at the Ministry and he came down to Letchworth. I managed to get him rooms out with some most charming friends, who were awfully good to Jacko. One afternoon, when we were waiting for tea on the lawn, I went back into the hotel to fetch some needlework, leaving Robbie and Jacko sitting in two deck-chairs and talking, their backs to me. I came back quietly across the grass, because when on grass I carried my shoes to avoid unnecessarily wearing them out, and I don't think they heard me. They were talking about something I had never heard of before and they called it heavy water.

I said nothing then, but that night, when we were going to bed, I asked Robbie about it.

He looked at me oddly, then said: 'Who's been talking to you? You'd better shut up.'

I said: 'But why? What is it?'

He just said, 'You shut up.'

I surmised that it was some nasty surprise that Herr Hitler had got niched for future use, and made a few enquiries amongst my more knowledgeable friends; their replies horrified me. But, I thought, the war will be over before they can start anything like that. It *must* be over.

That was very urgent.
It *must* be over.

August 2nd, 1944

I had quite the most violent headache all day and was washed
out by it. Churchill spoke in the House and he warned those who
could leave London to do so. These rocket shells seem to be sheer
horrors. I think—horrid as it is—I would much rather hear the
things coming.

August 6th, 1944

I had another dreadful headache, they are getting too much for
me. I don't know how to cope with them. There was a sudden
alert last night, but I was losing money at vingt-et-un and hardly
noticed it. My prisoners-of-war have heard the buzz that something is on. I can tell them nothing, save the sergeant who has
hatched up the code, and he gets the lot.
Pip is to be married to Iris on the 28th, and she seems a dear. I
couldn't go to Glasgow as I am so wretchedly ill, so they will
come here on their honeymoon.

August 8th, 1944

Really this was a most shocking night, talk about a noise! There
were a thousand bombers over us and the thunder they made
seemed to go on for half the night. Then there was a row in the
hotel itself. One of the men in the kitchen got very drunk and
chivvied a chambermaid round the great hall armed with a
bottle. I must say things do happen in this place. Whilst this was
going on I got out into the orchard and pinched the most
wonderful selection of apples for Robbie, who adores them.
Inside everyone was far too busy to bother about me.

Then there was a doodle-bug coming along, it came down Codicote way. It really was the most dreadful night.

August 13th, 1944

The Press is excited and prophesying that we are on the edge of great things. As an answer, Eisenhower has squashed all news being given out. We are now madly talking of peace again. Oh, how we want it! But the fact that we dare even speak of it is thrilling.

August 17th, 1944

At lunch time we learnt on the radio that we are surrounding Paris. This is marvellous. One almost wanted to stand up and sing the 'Marseillaise', which is a tune I love. Now we are all peace-happy, and who gives a damn for the bombs?

August 21st, 1944

They say Montgomery has told his men that the end of the war is within sight. I don't really suppose that he has done anything so silly, though some say he cannot keep his big mouth shut. Robbie said when he heard it: 'That's it. He would!'

August 22nd, 1944

The lunchtime radio told us that Paris has been liberated. That was the moment. Tonight the bells at Willian church, only a little way from this hotel, have been ringing, and the sound of them has been only too pleasant.

This came after a beastly day, for a bomb dropped much too close during breakfast, at the very moment when I was making up my mind to eat my tablespoonful of jam all in one whack and right now; or should I keep it for Sunday? The bomb came after a horrid night of explosions and gunfire, and this and that flying overhead. My knitting was going hard half the night, and if we get much more of this poor Mr. Levy's whisky will run out, which would be too bad. We can hardly believe that Paris is free.

August 25th, 1944

Paris, Aix and Avignon all free! *Sur le pont*, and all that. Just after breakfast two big planes flying in formation collided and came down in flames about six miles away, with all their bombs exploding here instead of at 'Ehren on the Rhein'. The ground seemed to rise up and shudder with it and I thought that the end of the world had come, though really I don't know if that would be quite so bad. The noise was deafening. It was one of the most awful experiences of the war and one I hope never to repeat.

August 28th, 1944

Pip's wedding day. He rang me up early and we had a talk, and then again after the wedding which apparently went off very well. They were going then to see a play *There Shall Be No Night*. (Well, well, well!) Now I am all agog to get this place nice for them. I have booked the ground floor bedroom in the old part.

August 29th, 1944

I collapsed with that awful pain again. I'm getting sick of this. It is so wretched knowing that it waits round the next corner for me and all the time.

August 31st, 1944

I got up early and tried to get the bedroom looking really nice for the bridal pair, but it is difficult getting sufficient flowers. I did it with all-white ones, and went over to Willian where I had some luck, for I got into a garden and helped myself to some white roses—for a very good cause.

Pip and Iris arrived tonight, both tired out after a dreadful journey, and by an earlier train than they had told us, so that there was no one to welcome them at the station, which was dreadful. So shocking for her.

September 4th, 1944

Brussels is free. It could perhaps be the end before winter, and this has been a wonderful thrill. At last hope has come, but when it does come one can hardly believe that it is true. The lethargy of a monotonous war running in phases like this is the most fatal part of it.

September 10th, 1944

When Robbie got down to lunch today he told me that the V.2's are really bad. One fell in Epping early this morning, and another in Chiswick. He says the report they make is quite deafening, though the harm no more than the buzz-bombs. It is rather a nasty thought.

There were few alerts in Letchworth really, but the ones that did come mattered a lot more than they had done in London, where in some odd way one got used to them. Then one afternoon the sky became alive above us. There were thousands of planes, and many towing other planes, which was new to us. The noise seemed to go on for ever.

September 17th, 1944

Dr. Obermer came down to see me again as the pain has been so much worse, and afterwards when we were walking in the garden together he tried to borrow money from me, a very large sum, too. I was absolutely shocked. It made me utterly miserable that he should have done this. I told him that I could not do it. News has come that we have invaded Holland with our first paratroop army. Thousands of planes, the ones apparently which went over yesterday and a long time into the night, landed them at Arnhem. Now I gather they can cross the Rhine here and get into Germany by the back door, like the Huns on the bulge in the line.

September 19th, 1944

This invasion, if it goes well, should bring the end of the war weeks earlier, and break this winter. I am not at all sure though that it is going well. There seems a reserve about the news which is ominous.

September 22nd, 1944

Hatfield caught it last night. These things are coming a darned sight too near.

Everybody thought that now the war would end by Christmas, perhaps even by mid-October. The Government released its demobilization plans, which gave the future a real kick and increased our faith in an early ending. Even if the V.2's were coming over madly, and they were, it seemed that on the dawn of a new day peace might come. By the 25th news was beginning to leak out. It had been very tough going at Arnhem, for apparently the onslaught was disclosed. The old spy game! This news coming at the end of the war, when we had felt that now we were nearly through, was a disaster.

Robbie was deeply worried.

He was not happy about the fact that night after night there were alerts and alarms, not to mention those infernal 'things that go bump in the night'. In the Ministry he had been talking with a girl friend who came from Farnborough way. There had been no trouble there at all and she suggested that there were several nice hotels in the neighbourhood, why not move down there?

Until this time I had never even heard of Frimley where eventually I went. She recommended The Prior's Kitchen as a hotel that was different and where we would be happy, and we arrived there one hot September afternoon with little idea of what to expect. It was one of those lovely days that come at that time of year. The station was quiet, and the little main street we walked up was old-fashioned and friendly. The Prior's Kitchen was a big old mansion and far more private house than hotel; in it the two daughters had grown into the middle years and now ran it as an hotel.

It was big and spacious, and if the bedrooms were small the sitting-rooms were larger and the food amazingly good, considering the times in which we lived. We had tea on the lawn, and Gypsy the pony walked along and pinched all the cucumber sandwiches when I wasn't looking.

'I shall like this place,' I thought. 'It's very much me.'

Soldiers waited at meals; with a touch of genius they had managed to employ young men from a medical school at Aldershot. They were the try-outs for new cures, offering themselves as guinea pigs for shorter hours and more fun. Most of them were on a mosquito-biting programme, I gathered, to do with the treatment of malaria. The idea was to get yourself well and truly bitten and then the docs. learnt from it. Every night when they came in to wait at table they would on enquiry roll up their sleeves in triumph and show you their mosquito bites.

The Misses Mason ran the hotel and with them a friend I had known as a child at Frinton. It was happy-go-lucky. Nobody would have been at all surprised whatever you did, and certainly they would never have complained. They let me do their flowers for them, and I arranged big dishes of autumn leaves, pebbles, and those small red fungi from the woods. A soldier and girl came in to tea, and she looked at these and said, '*Don't they do them mushrooms nice?*' One of my greatest compliments.

There was of course nothing to do.

When I had finished work and had a break I just walked in the country. Early on I discovered Field Lane, and when I had done the unending letters I went there. There were attractive woods—the pine trees and the late glow of gorse—and about it that soft yet acrid Surrey scent.

Robbie took against the train service, which I admit was difficult. However, on September 30th we had one joyous piece of news for the English took the long range guns which had been knocking hell out of Dover. Now the white cliffs had at last gone quiet. But if Dover was quiet, we were not. All day long, and all night too, the tanks rattled crazily through Frimley in a continuous trail.

The taking of Calais had been a great thing, abroad we had had all sorts of successes, but at the same time the end of the war seemed no nearer. At this time one realized that only peace could relax one.

October 3rd, 1944

A long working day laden with letters and then had to telephone a complete thousand-word article to the *Daily Sketch*, with half the lounge listening. I think they thought I'd gone mad and could not dream what was on the other end. It was an article on religion, of all things, and the giggles of cadets and their girls nearly killed me. I went over to see Camberley. Too Poona-Poona for me.

October 6th, 1944

Two nights of nasty alerts and aircraft everywhere. I think the Huns get the buzz of where we are. They have a down on us. This house is old and ramshackle with nowhere to go, and glass all over the place. I don't think the people know what glass can do. Unfortunately I do. They are charming folks here, and the *bonne camaraderie* is tremendous. Tonight one of the soldier waiters was most depressed. Mosquitoes won't bite him. Tomorrow he'll be out. What a consternation!

Robbie came down on a three days' holiday, to get some sleep, but the tanks were too shocking, and going night and day; and on the third morning when he could find no way of passing the time he asked, 'But what do you *do* here?'

If I did not write and tire myself out that way, I admitted, there would be nothing to do.

He said: 'We ought to get out of this. Those tanks, and now the alerts. We ought to go.'

October 12th, 1944

We left Frimley today and came down to Hove which on the face of things seems idiotic, but here all aircraft pass over the coast line and it is quieter. Besides, they have no tanks, and there are things to do.

I met Leonora Eyles early on, and she finally got us established in the right hotel, though for a short time we had a very unpleasant period of trying to find somewhere to settle in. Of course there was lots to do and that *did* help.

October 20th, 1944

Toilet rolls are now almost off the market and causing a worry which is coming to everyone. The shortage of elastic (we have not been able to buy this for quite a long time) has put several people into a panic, and it was suggested that the time would come when ladies had to forswear their knickers. Could be. But this is not the answer to the other worry.

Brighton has quite a different life, of the type I have not known

N

since war came. It is escape. One can go out here and have coffee and elevenses with a ladies' orchestra playing *Salut d'Amour*, and that is unbelievable. There is a big choice of cinemas. There is much that is a joy and a relaxation at the time we most need it.

October 25th, 1944

This would happen to me!
I get down here where nothing has dropped since 1940, and what happens? Here it comes, boys!
In the evening there was an alert and we went down into the basement bar of the hotel where we are staying. There came seven of those mighty crumps in the distance, Shoreham way, and we came to the conclusion that the Huns had realized where we were.
Too bad.

October 26th, 1944

The headaches are ghastly.

*   *   *

With October ended we realized that any chance of finishing the war with the year had gone. We should have to slog on through the winter to the spring, perhaps yet another of those awful springs which had shattered all of us.

The hotel where we now were fed us well, how I cannot think, for the points were narrowing all the time, though perhaps they had a Hen in the background of their lives. The Hen did the weekly wash for me, we posted it to and fro. I got brief letters from her.

I had news that in the new year I should be a grandmother, which was exciting, but most of us were deeply depressed that Arnhem had failed and it had been such a valiant effort which had

ost us too much. The V.2's continued to drop on London and I
lived always in a state of jagged nerves lest I should never see
Robbie again.

November 14th, 1944

A ghastly rumour is going the rounds that Herr Hitler has a V.3
weapon up his sleeve, a real beauty which has a shell that will
freeze you to death. What a thought! I remember hearing Robbie
and Jacko talking about the thing they called 'heavy water', and
wonder if this is connected.
But by now I have realized that it is futile to ask questions of
Robbie. Talk about the clam! There is quite a lot of evidence that
might back the persistent rumour that Hitler is dead. We have
reached now another period when nothing ever happens. In this
war it is always too much or nothing, and both are vile.
I nearly passed out on Brighton station today with a shocking
headache. This is hell.

November 15th, 1944

The rumour persists that Hitler is dead, and they say that Goering
died with him. Possibly they had some unshareable plan to get
away, and the chaps who couldn't go with them bumped them
off? That is an idea. Nothing would surprise me. In fact it is my
one big surprise that he did not die years ago.

A year before the war broke out I had had an experience
which had alarmed and interested me a lot. I receive a daily fan
mail, which I answer patiently. A woman asked to see me. I
never see anyone till I know what they want, but she was pressing. She wanted to tell me something about Herr Hitler. She said
that she felt that to save the world from the coming war it was the
duty of someone—and it might be easier for a woman than for a
man—to make the final move, and she had a plan.

In the end we met one morning in the Strand Palace Hotel. She was educated, quiet, and well born; and we selected a corner away from the others. A lot of people coming off night duty were about the place and I chose somewhere well aloof. She was a small woman in the thirties and shortly leaving for Munich. She had the ticket with her. She told me that she had the means of getting into the Nest at Berchtesgarten, and was going out there with the intention of murdering Hitler because she believed if he died the war could be averted. She argued that one woman should be prepared to give her life to save the world.

She amazed me. She was completely sincere.

As we talked two men came away from the more general crowd of the lounge and sat down at the table next to us. I knew they did it deliberately, with an overdone casualness towards the two of us. I rose.

As we walked out I glanced back from the door and I saw them watching us. Outside the hotel she told me that she would send me a single line when she got to Munich. She promised that. I warned her of the men; she said things like that did not worry her, she expected them, they had to be.

I went home with no fixed ideas about this, I thought that I could trust her, but one can never be too sure. Three days later I received an unsigned postcard from Munich, with a picture of their war memorial. Nothing more.

I never did hear anything more.

I did not think that there was anything she could do to stop the war, though she had thought this, and if her life went it was, alas, sacrificed in vain, but she had her ideals and one admires anyone for that.

November 22nd, 1944

After all there is a tremendous push going on in Holland, and we are told this will work. Later reports say the weather has worsened: in spite of all the ideas about weather ships and so on,

I don't think they are so awfully clever. We have had so little luck with the weather.

November 28th, 1944

There has been a ghastly explosion in a bomb store near Burton-on-Trent, and I fear a tremendous loss of life. What a shocking thing war is and one never becomes used to its tragedies. I wish one could.

*   *   *

December came in with a very cold spell, and the *Sunday Dispatch* prophesied the return of the Luftwaffe for December 10th. A mine blew up in Kemp Town with an almighty bang, and again there was this feeling of tenseness and of apprehension. One was aware of something going on. It was in the air.

December 19th, 1944

The Huns have dropped a surprise packet on us in the way of a giant offensive and to our horror they have actually fought their way twenty miles on. This is something in the nature of a Christmas present, isn't it? We are all terribly worried for if they break through now they could keep this wretched war going on for months longer.

Goodness only knows what has happened out there. There is close secrecy for security purposes, and all news has been squashed.

December 20th, 1944

Although little is admitted we understand that the Huns have made heavy penetrations through our lines, and are coming on fast. We were led to believe that this could not happen. I bet it is six months on to the war. How dreadful!

December 21st, 1944

The news horrifying.
Now it is thought that they may send their paratroops over here to drop an Arnhem on us when we are all unaware. If they have any sense they will risk everything to bust us.
Nothing in the shops.
One has hardly the heart for Christmas presents.

December 22nd, 1944

News worse, and you would have thought that by now the British had grown used to bad news.
The Hen sending back the laundry pencilled a note saying she knew what she would do with the whole bloody lot, and somebody ought to do it, why not she and me?
Why not?
Eisenhower says that we may by courage turn this into a tremendous victory, but we've heard that one before. In the main this is a cigarette Christmas because there is nothing else to buy.

Christmas Day, 1944

The hotel tried so hard to make it a success and gave us a marvellous dinner with real nuts, the first we have seen for ages. It is very cold and all of us afraid to turn on the news. Mr. Churchill is said to be in Athens.

December 31st, 1944

A new year comes in at midnight.

The slight improvement in the war news has given us that fresh hope we clutch at so feverishly, and it is pathetic the way we do this.

I want to write this tonight, alone in my room, for I feel strangely about the year that is coming.

I am sure it will end the war, but I believe that there is another war with us, one already deeply rooted in men's hearts, and this will not be ended. I want to record this now. Later people will only think that I have invented and enlarged on it.

I have watched a change coming in the hearts of our people, and this frightens me. In 1914–18 we lost our fervent patriotism; we began that war fighting only for England, and we ended it fighting only for ourselves. I think there may easily be some rising, some sort of civil war here, which I pray may be bloodless but which will achieve its own quite desperate end of destroying people as we have known them.

I want to see everyone happy, because I love people, but now they are too much for themselves. I hate poverty and sickness and pain, but these things—these human sufferings—could very well be the barbs which have urged us on to greater glory. Without incentive, hearts wither. This is what I fear most. That lethargy of confidence which could come.

Tonight I believe that the right incentives are already dead in our hearts, we have not been strong enough to hold them fast. For God, for King and Country seems tired. Home matters more. A clever man said tonight when we were talking of the new year, 'Yes, but it will be peace.' I am not so sure. *Will* it be the real peace, the peace born of love and happiness together?

Of course it won't. We have already committed ourselves.

12

For what can war but endless war still breed?
MILTON

A DENSE FOG hung over England and there were rumours of trouble in Budapest, but where was there not trouble just then? It was the static time at home that comes after Christmas, when it seems that the new year will never break or the first flowers come.

I was additionally miserable on January 5th when I learnt that a V.2. had landed on part of the Royal Chelsea Hospital. The war days of gallant old men being done, it seemed horrible that this could happen. The last time I had been there a charming one of them had shown me round the chapel, when an alert came. He said he thought I ought to go home, came with me to the gate, and wished me well. Then calmly he told me: 'Men who have been in the Army most of their lives get used to war. It never happens that a shell hits *you*, and that's something.'

I had gone home rejoicing on that, with the guns blazing and heaven only knows what overhead. I thought of that man when I got the news, he had seemed young to be a pensioner, and when I had said this he had smiled and said, 'I was lucky for I stepped into a dead man's shoes.' He was killed that day when the V.2 did hit him.

★　　★　　★

Hotel life can be bitterly lonely, and most of my time was spent typing in my room. I had a lot of work for which I thanked heaven, for this job is one when you have nothing and are desperate, or have everything and are desperate still!

January 18th, 1945

Cracov and Czestochowa have been taken and we are told that Russia anticipates actually crossing into the Reich today. I wonder if the old rumour that they were promised to be the first nation in Berlin is true?

A terrible gale is blowing, and out in the streets of Brighton people are almost being swept away. V.2's continue to drop on London, it is so worrying for Robbie.

January 19th, 1945

It is intensely cold again and this really is a very stark winter, with such a lot of snow. Today the whole length of the Avenue in Hove is white and glittering. Like this it is much too far for Robbie to walk to Brighton station.

The Swedes have told us that the V.2's will get bigger. No nation seems to know when to keep its big mouth shut.

I should have thought that the story of Napoleon, a history which I believe Hitler has studied very closely, would have taught him that Russia is not easily overwhelmed. Lodz fell today.

Imagine my surprise when at lunch I found a whole (real) orange on my table, the first that I have seen for ages, and this most kind hotel gave one to each of its residents. It *was* a surprise, but of course I could not possibly eat it. I just look at it. I wonder if I shall live to see a real banana again. I ate my last in 1939, and with tears.

January 22nd, 1945

I went up to London and a V.2 dropped fairly near with the most shattering noise that I have ever heard. It snowed all the way, and the gale has been dreadful. Everywhere there are posters about the Ruskies ending the war, for somehow or other we seem to be bogged down in Holland (something shocking must have happened there) and we are getting nowhere.

The sense of restlessness and what I might call inner apprehension seems to be with us all. It is difficult to cope with creative work in this mood.

The newspapers said that as the armies of Russia drew nearer to the capital the Berliners were evacuating. We speculated as to what Herr Hitler and his friends would do. He was said to be in the Bunker and Eva Braun with him. People have said he was in love with her, which I should have thought dubious, I never suspected that he was woman-minded but maybe I had been wrong all along.

Ever since the bomb outrage when he was so badly wounded, but unhappily not killed, the photographs which got through showed him very much altered. One arm seemed to be almost useless, and I gathered that at times he stuttered, walking more like a marionette compelled by wires than of his own accord. One thing I was convinced was sure, he would never let himself be taken alive.

All along there had been the occasional reports of riots in Germany, but whether these were true or the result of wishful thinking we did not know. These people must have become listless, as indeed we also had. Bombing, and the eternal continuation of a war, with the bad food and the semi-starvation which it must produce, bear as a fruit this lethargy which is perhaps war's worst inheritance.

February 3rd, 1945

Now for the first time the Berliners must be hearing the sound of Stalin's guns, and I imagine with real horror. They say that the Bunker under the Chancellery is a hive of action, but who really knows? Hitler and his high-ups and Fräulein Eva Braun are all snug down there. I should have thought it much more probable that they would have fitted themselves up with some vigorous submarine with the idea of a flight to the Argentine, or somewhere equally safe. I can see nothing else for Hitler except to go off into retirement, disappear, and emerge three years ahead as the Messiah Lady Kenilworth said he could have been. If he dated that return just before World War 3 he might get a hearing.

February 4th, 1945

Berlin must be a terrible shambles for we are sending mighty forces over to bombard from the air. Whole streets burst into flame, far worse than anything we have ever had here and ours has been bad enough. It is soul-eating. This doling out of wholesale agony to innocents is so shocking.

Robbie and I walked in the gardens of Palmeira Square and saw the little bulbs all spiking up; you'd have thought the quite vicious snows would put them back, but nothing ever does. Spring comes again.

February 6th, *1945*

The Big Three are in conference somewhere in the Crimea, and a plane with many of Mr. Churchill's staff in it crashed. These planes are not as safe as they try to make out. One of these days someone really great will go for six, then we shall wake up to that.

Another big rumour is going the rounds (we live on rumours), saying that we are starting another big offensive in the west. A bit early in the year for that, surely?

The new phase had begun. The moment the V.2's ended Robbie said I could return to London. The Hen learning this wrote in great jubilation. She would, she said, keep her eyes skinned for this and have everything ready.

February 9th, *1945*

Montgomery has started another offensive round Arnhem (yet another! Goodness, how sick we are of being afraid for the men!), and we all hope that it will go well, because this *could* be the last. We always say this.

February 10th, *1945*

There was heavy gunfire last night, and an imminent danger warning also, yet in spite of the noise nothing actually happened. There seems now to be a general hotting-up of gunfire, and there are crunches coming every now and then from the sea, once in the middle of the night it sounded as if a whole cartload of bombs was being dropped into it. Funny-peculiar, I'd say.

February 12th, 1945

The conference in the Crimea has now ended.

February 14th, 1945

This has been quite the most beautiful springtime day, a true St. Valentine, with bits and pieces out in the gardens and I sat out in the sunshine. Just as Robbie got into London a dreadful V.2 fell on Oxford Circus with heavy loss of life. At this stage of the war you would have thought we should have stopped this.

February 17th, 1945

A film of the conference in the Crimea has just been shown, and when I saw it I was appalled. I should never have known President Roosevelt and he must be a very sick man. He sat there with a shawl, or what looked like a shawl, round him; he was like some poor old woman, deathly thin, his eyes sunken into hollows, and I should have said that he was dying. To lose him now would be horrible. The others were all chattering and apparently not noticing anything amiss, but this poor man looked to be tragically sick.

If the buzz-bombs have gone for ever, these V.2's haven't.

February 24th, 1945

The big push is said to have started at dawn, and they hope to get back to the line. We have had so many set-backs that one is almost afraid to hope for this time. Montgomery is in charge, I gather, and although he looks rather like a ferret my experience of ferrets would tell me that they are darned good hangers-onners.

February 25th, 1945

We have pushed five miles on a twenty-two-mile front, which conveys little to me but must be good. Tonight there was a rumour that we were fifteen miles from Cologne, and if so this has indeed shaken somebody. The bother in war is that so often there is too much talk, so that when you have had it some years you don't believe the truth when it comes.

By the 28th we knew that we were actually shelling Cologne, and felt as everyone else did that now we had only to cross the Rhine for the Germans to lay down their arms. May 4th was predicted as being the likely day for an armistice, even by the people who knew. I had been told too many armistice days that were certs to believe another word.

Meanwhile I suffered an accident.

I went into a very dark cinema in Brighton, the girl had no torch, tried to bustle me into a seat, and never mentioned a step there was. I tripped and fell on to the iron arm of a tip-up chair. The pain was for a moment excruciating. I sat there for a time, not daring to move lest I fainted, and half an hour later tottered out and home in a taxi. I had broken a couple of ribs. The doctor said that I must claim on the cinema, which seemed tough, I thought; but the girl had been over-casual and in the end I appealed to them.

There was the usual argument, the doctor's certificate, and I was to think of recompense. I wanted the bill paid, of course, and I rather thought a permit allotting me free entry to any of their chain of cinemas would be heaven. One of their gentlemen came down to see me. He was persuasive, charming, never denying that they were in the wrong, though when I asked for recompense he looked distressed. I mentioned the fact that they were paying the bills so they realized that it was their responsibility; what about my loss of working hours?

He thought for a moment, then he told me that he had something quite miraculous in his car and went outside the door into the Avenue to fetch it to show me. There was a moment when I thought in terms of the mink coat, then quenched my ambitions. When he returned he did, however, nearly knock me over with amazement, for he brought with him two great fat yellow grapefruit. He had, he said, got a whole case in his dicky.

Now I had not seen one of these since 1939, and had forgotten how delectable they were. Now, seeing them, I wanted them more than anything else in the world. I laid down my arms and accepted them, and I should like to say here and now that they were the most beautiful things that I have ever eaten.

'Gosh! You're mad!' said Robbie when told. 'A few grape-fruit, and knocked about the way you were! You could have asked for anything, what did you think you were doing?'

I spoke the truth when I said, 'Well, I don't really think I know.'

★   ★   ★

March 6th, 1945

Cologne fell today.
I pray only that those twin towers of the Gothic cathedral stand secure, because they are so beautiful, and I should hate to think of that place with the ravages of war on it. Robbie says that when we get farther into Germany I can return home. I got my wardrobe trunk out today. . . . *Today!*

March 7th, 1945

Now the V.2's have hotted up again, Balham and Tooting. I am so upset when I think of Robbie in the M. of I. all day, because sooner or later he is bound to get something nasty.
Meanwhile I shopped for my stepmother Jo who is dying of the cold at Stratford. She wanted combinations with high necks and

long sleeves, and never having heard of such things I set forth. Believe it or not, I got them at Hannington's. *With* high necks and long sleeves! The girl who served me looked upon me as a gift from God, I imagine, and had given up all thought of ever getting a customer for them. I bought three and a couple of the most ghastly nighties as well, with long cuffed sleeves and high necks and pockets.

March 8th, 1945

Whilst I was buying those appalling combinations for Jo, and laughing myself sick over them, we crossed the Rhine. And I had always thought that when this hour came I should be so carried away by it that I should be praying hard in some church.

Of course Winston Churchill was there. I suppose we should all have been wildly enthusiastic about it all, but perhaps the victory had come a little too late. It did that in 1918, when I remember I stood helplessly and asked 'Is the war really over?' and then said 'Fancy that!' as though it didn't matter any more.

Allied with our crossing the Rhine there came a dire V.2 on to Smithfield Market at the busiest time; it killed many, and our rations went west for a whole month ahead, so that we were back on bully and Icelandic cod and all those other nasties with which rationing was eked out.

We gathered that overseas the Army was progressing moderately well. Most of my time was spent on the bed, for the ribs hurt a great deal, and now I had full time to spare lying there and kicking myself for having been such a fool over those silly grapefruit.

Why did I do it? I have asked myself that question time and time again in my life. Why, oh why? Perhaps the trouble was that I have always been passionately fond of fruit, and although Robbie said it would have been better if I had been fond of gin, because then he too would have got something out of it, I didn't think he was right.

March 14th, 1945

There were a lot of horrible explosions in the night and I hated every moment of it. This morning people say that these noises come because we are blowing up Dunkirk, though I don't feel this can be right. Planes are everywhere, and my headache in one of its worst spells when nothing conquers it. I cannot think why one person has to suffer quite so much, quite so often and quite so badly.

March 17th, 1945

Mother's birthday and inside myself I always feel I must celebrate it a little. Dr. Obermer coming down here to see me tomorrow.

For a week the headaches were appalling, though now I told myself that I should take fresh heart, for we were nearing that last spring with victory at hand, and then surely something could be done for me when the really good doctors came back.

March 22nd, 1945

There is a report that the Ruhr is on fire. Well, now they know how we liked the city of London burning. War is such a cruel thing for in it whole nations are victimized by the few. I don't suppose that the German man in the street really wanted this war. Mainz is ours.

How we can have got that far I cannot imagine, and now we are waiting for Monty's final move. Winston bobbed across the Rhine in a boat. He would! Surely one of these days some Hun will get him if he goes on taking these risks.

o

March 27th, 1945

The news is marvellous, we forge ahead, but there is news here which is even greater. Believe it or not, the beaches are going to be opened for Easter! It is dreadful to think that with us is a generation of little children who have never had the chance to play on a beach, or have a nice paddle; everywhere has been mined.

The night before last, they say, V.2's dropped every twenty-five minutes on London, and Robbie looked so grey and drawn when he got down here. If this war lasts much longer I am sure many of us will break down.

Easter Sunday, April 1st, 1945

I lunched at Sweeting's with D. A. Clarke-Smith, the most engaging host, and the food was the usual, I am afraid. No restaurant can help this and it is wonderful how they manage at all.

There has been a black-out in the war news, nobody knows anything, unless Robbie does, and he will never talk. The V.2's come over which is something I cannot understand when we are inland beyond the Rhine. Clarkie thinks this is the last three weeks of the war.

April 6th, 1945

Robbie says that soon I can go home. I wrote and told the Hen, so she will be out on the scrounge for me, bless her heart. For the moment London is still dangerous, and I am weak from eternal headaches, and weary too of the country life. Here there is none of the stimulation that I need. We took a car out into the country today, near Poynings, and in the woods the windflowers were out. It was so beautiful.

April 17th, 1945

It is very hot weather. Robbie looks so ill and tired, he needs a long night's rest for this business of every-other-night-sleeping is so daft.

The big explosions seem still to be going on out at sea, and we can't think why. The beaches are clear, and the children of a new generation just don't know what to do with sand and water. The shops have dug out all the old spades and pails put by for the duration, but I have yet to see the water-wings coming up. Now, attached to the wires of the sunblinds above the pavements, buckets chatter together and spades swing.

This *is* something.

April 22nd, 1945

We went out to the woods and gathered bluebells today and for the first time I heard the cuckoo.

Always in my life this is *the* day of the year. The cuckoo. Tonight I came to London, home after all. I cannot believe that it is true and I wanted to break down and cry. I feel almost too happy to be back.

In bobbed the Hen. ' 'ello! 'ow's Madam?' Usually she refuses to come on a Sunday night, but did this time, actually rushing her brown ale at the Lord Nelson to do it. She indicated Germany with a contemptuous jerk of her head. 'They ain't 'arf catching it now,' said the Hen as she plonked down two stout packets of 'gran.' on the kitchen table. 'And if you 'ad a mite of tea . . . ?' There is no place like home and it has not changed.

13

War buys scars.
PROVERB

April 23rd, 1945

We are told that Berlin is falling fast, but that this will see only
the end of the war in Europe, and there will still be the East to be
conquered. I am disappointed. I had forgotten the Japs.

Obviously everything was hurrying up now, and the Russians
and the Americans met on the Elbe. Berlin was in chaos. All sorts
of stories went the rounds about Herr Hitler. He was still
supposed to be in the Bunker under the Chancellery which was
quite impervious to shelling. There were other stories, one that he
had been seen in Danzig boarding a submarine and some of his

212

friends with him. The unmistakable Goering, and that little squirt Goebbels. I could not believe that a man like Hitler would commit himself to death without making a bid to escape, but maybe I was wrong.

He had always said that if he lost the war it would be the end of the world. On the other hand, if he won it, it would mean a thousand years of peace in Europe. He was violently antagonistic to the Russians. I rather respected his foresight in some ways, I felt that he had the gift of this; but he could not have really meant the end of the world.

April 28th, 1945

Today it actually snowed, which was a surprise. We went down to Lamorbey. A few months ago they had a bomb in the grounds at the head of the lake, which looked horribly naked and dim and exposed. The kitchen garden wall was down, the trees dead. Yet still the daffodils flowered.
We are told that Herr Himmler has sued for peace, but won't surrender to the Russians, which means that it is just worthless. However, the end cannot be very far away.

Sunday, April 29th, 1945

People are saying that Musso was shot recently in Milan or near Milan, and with him a woman he had lived with for some time, and who had bolted with him. They were taken out, persuaded that they would be helped to escape, and then betrayed. He, too glad to take what he believed was the road to safety, went with the men who suggested security. He was driven away in a car, stopped in the country and both of them turned out, then slugged. To me this seems terrible, but all along this has been a terrible war. One hates treachery whoever dies for it.
I suppose the news is true, on second thoughts? I seem to remember that Musso has already died many times.

April 30th, 1945

We are being told that peace will come tomorrow. Nobody knows when we shall be told, or what will actually happen. The curious thing is that there is still this frightful apathy everywhere, even with the Hen, which is unusual (no Union Jack in the button-hole). This is worse than the day when the war began, and the mulberry tree at Moreton smelt of sunlit leaves.

It is snowing now.

Is this the winter of our discontent?

May 1st, 1945

Peace was a flop.

It never arrived as advertised. Really, this is an idiotic war and all the flags have come down and that's that.

May 2nd, 1945

They broke in on the wireless tonight at 10.30, to say that Berlin fell this afternoon. All sorts of stories are going round about Hitler, one even that he was married, which I should have thought was the last thing that he would have done.

Now a few wilted flags are up, looking rather out of place in a bombed city. None of this war has gone to pattern if you ask me, and everyone is so dead sick of it that they cannot even approach peace with joy.

We are cold at heart.

May 4th, 1945

Half Germany is surrendering tomorrow (always tomorrow, never jam today), and we've lost interest. It is reported that Goebbels is dead, having committed suicide in the Bunker after killing his children, then someone else says he was shot in flight.

We stand looking into the eyes of peace. Could it be that they are hollow?

They say it could be tomorrow. At the latest, Tuesday.

Every entry and every remark centred round the one enquiry 'Will it be today?' We were warned to be sure to get sufficient bread in, for the moment peace was declared all the shops would shut (I have no idea why) and nobody knew when they would open again. This information sent every housewife scurrying out. I got a bottle of whisky with agility from the shop, saying my husband would beat me if I went home with nothing. The man was most sympathetic. Robbie, however, was furious with me when I got home and told him about it. I thought he would think it rather amusing.

May 8th, V.E. Day, 1945

This is it.

It is very thundery and there is not a single taxi on the streets. Nobody can go anywhere. Every shop is shut and this is like Christmas Day in the workhouse. Talk about an anti-climax, this is the one!

There are hordes of 'oiks' wandering the streets, the usual percentage of drunks, but you can't blame them for that. There are occasional bombers overhead, and I feel that as a peace it is downright depressing.

But the first floodlighting has returned and that looks fine. People had fireworks saved. The idea of the crowds is to go car-rocking, and I believe Piccadilly Circus has been a shocker for this. They rock the car till they turn you over. Enormous crowds at the Palace.

May 10th, 1945

This is the first normal day since peace came in an abnormal world.

May 11th, 1945

I had to do a broadcast today and never thought that I could get there for we have no petrol left and there are no taxis, and with my foot I cannot walk that distance.

No vehicles being allowed to us has made rejoicing impossible. Give me war!

There had been none of the eager rejoicing of 1918 when we had really believed that war had been removed for ever. Now we never thought that for a moment. Perhaps this was the most wretched part of a victory that was ice-cold. There is a limit to human endurance and we had had too much; we were not the same people who had gone out to fight. Perhaps the best of us had gone.

Even on the thanksgiving Sunday, when the King and Queen went to St. Paul's to give thanks, the weather took the opportunity to break and it poured half the time.

*   *   *

Now my prisoners-of-war were returning home.

They flew in on a bright day, having had my letters telling them guest rooms would be ready for them and they must come to me—almost a stranger—as a relation waiting to welcome them. One after another they appeared at the flat, these strangers yet not strangers—to whom I had written for so long. Men I knew from a sheet of notepaper, and now met. I liked so much the New Zealander to whom I had written for the longest time, and who had been in the most hopeless camp of all. He told me it had been utterly dreadful and during the last year he had not been able to sleep; he thought at any moment death might come.

When I took him to his guest room I offered him a couple of Soneril to sleep on. He looked at me with suspicion and I realized that he mistrusted the help, for he had grown to mistrust everything. Then almost ashamedly he said: 'I'm sorry. You get awfully nervy after the type of life I have had lately.' Furtively he kept looking behind him for what he called the Ferrets (guards).

He was amazed at my shoes. I took him into Burton Court grounds, apologizing that I could not walk on the gravel path because the soles of my shoes let it in. He said if he had known that my shoes were so bad he would have pinched some for me. The German women were not one bit as shabby as we were; I think we horrified him, and it would have been a joy to pinch their things.

However, he did take the Soneril and that night slept nobly, and came to breakfast looking much better. He became like a son of the house. We thought of him as that.

May 17th, 1945

I have been better today and perhaps with the war ending I can get some real relief. I would not have believed that anyone could have felt so ill and still live.

There is the sick underlying feeling that things are not right with the Ruskies. I hate it but it is everywhere. I cannot think what can have happened.

May 19th, 1945

Food is almost unprocurable.

Winston Churchill did warn us this would happen, and now even that Icelandic cod has gone, which, like the poor, was always with us. The Hen is baffled. But she has an eye on a half-leg of lamb she knows.

They say everything will be better when Japan caves in. This now seems to be the longest spring of them all.

V.E. Day had improved nothing, and all along we had looked

to it with such hope. Now we looked for the next peace day. For
what?

★   ★   ★

With the dawning of June a general election hung over us;
rather rushed, we thought. The weather was coldly damp and
quite unlike summertime, with that lethargy of wars till with us.
Robbie would stay on at the M. of I. only until the final peace
day, when his job ended.

June 9th, 1945

It is a curious thing that, this war coming to its end, we really
know little of what happened to Hitler and Eva Braun. He
married her two days before he shot himself, it is said. The reports
are confused and mixed. Goebbels poisoned his children, then in
another room himself and his wife, yet one paper had a photo-
graph of them all lying dead in the same room. I think Hitler has
got away.
Dante won the Derby and of course the Hen was on it. She is
racing wise, learning tips in her Dad's 'gents' on Epsom race-
course, so she says.

June 15th, 1945

Raspberries to make jam at 7/6 a lb.! However, I did lift a pork
pie in with a cauliflower at the greengrocer's.

★   ★   ★

The election began.
Our old friend from Letchworth Lewis May put up for a
Camberwell constituency against Mrs. Freda Corbett (Labour)
of the L.C.C., and I went down there to help him. I *would* pick

myself a seat next to a vigorous prize-fighter only too anxious to have a row—and he got it in a generous free-for-all. There were rumours that Labour would win the election, going on the Forces' votes coming in from overseas. I could not believe this, for every one of us owed our lives to Winston Churchill and should have known it. What a repayment if it swung the wrong way!

When Robbie was on duty I went into the back streets of Chelsea to hear our own candidate speaking out of the back of a van. The Hen joined me. She was, amongst other things, and always had been, a violent Conservative, and she had not been with me five minutes before a drunken bluejacket started a disturbance. He had not the wits to keep his feet, however, and fell into the gutter where he lay, when the Hen hopped along and kicked him. I was horrified. I went to the Hen and tried to pull her off him, when the man in the most obscene language accused me of having done it myself.

The whole situation looked very ugly, I could hardly accuse the Hen, but was not called upon to do this. The gallant old lady turned round in a fury. 'What, 'er?' said she. 'She never done nothink. I did it. Me!'

*   *   *

June 26th, 1945

Death comes slowly, and this pain is killing me. I long for direction but there is none. I think I must have done something vile in another incarnation and am paying for it now. With interest.

On July 2nd I went into the King's Road and saw Winston Churchill. He looked smaller than before, changed, as he sat on the lowered hood of a car, his face strange but his eyes shrewd.

I came to the conclusion that things were not going well, and electioneering in Camberwell looked awfully like it. Only the previous night a young woman had kicked up a fuss at a meeting. She could not get biscuits for her baby. She had the baby with her and I must say that she did not seem particularly fond of it by the way she treated it. I suggested that she could bake bread in the oven to make biscuits, and she gave me a look. 'What, me?' she asked, and then contemptuously: 'Think I'd take that trouble for the little bastard? No b——y fear!'

If this woman in Camberwell was representative of the new world, one thing stood out clearly: We were going to lose the peace, and in a big way.

It was at this time that I made an entry which I quote now because looking back I recognize some foresight in my anxiety for the future.

'I write this now because I have to write it. The future of the world worries me so desperately. I felt like this with the new year. It is worse now.

'This election has brought me face to face with the people of a changed world, and I am afraid. These are the people who could forswear the standards by which for generations we have abided.

'Can we afford to lose our greatness now?

'We are going to lose it.

'Ahead change lies, and from the ruins of this country there could come a generation that may even set aside its faith. I am truly afraid for a path which it seems we could tread into a future which no man wishes to step into. I am so afraid.'

We were approaching the end.

The election was over, its interest paling, for we had to wait a solid month before the Forces' votes could be counted. By that time the anti-climax had arrived, and when we knew the truth I believe Winston Churchill said, 'But they can't do this to me!'

They could. And they did.

*   *   *

I think the brutal truth is that it would have been better in the long run if we had been invaded and maybe from that horror we could have learnt a greater lesson.

On August 2nd of the peace year my first grandson was born, and following close on that come the last three entries in my diary. Entries of despair:

August 6th, 1945

We have a bomb that splits the atom, and we have dropped it on Hiroshima in Japan.
The news came through on the radio tonight, and for a moment we were almost paralysed with sheer abhorrence.
We dropped it.
This is the end of the world as we have known it. It could be the end of ourselves.

August 7th, 1945

The response of England to the dropping of the atom bomb has been one of horror. We all talked of it and hated it. We realized then that from now on none of us need hope to die in bed, and even if thousands of the fighting services had to die if we didn't drop it, I still think that all will ultimately perish because we did drop it.
Sometimes I wonder if God meant us to know this much, meant us to interfere with His planning of the world. By moving ahead at such speed, and tapping His secrets, do we not bring ourselves closer to the day which He called Judgment Day and which is really the annihilation of a world?
Perhaps I ought not to think this way, and should be ashamed of myself, but my own thoughts shock me now at the end of the war.

August 10th, 1945

The Japs are surrendering. They could not take the bomb which we saw fit to drop. I know the Americans actually let it go, but the partnership was connected with it, and surely some of the fault was ours? Now all the paper chains and the tired flags mean nothing. I for one would have rather gone on than have dropped this bomb, and I still think it a blot on our history from which we can never escape in the future.

Amidst the rather half-hearted rejoicing—nothing like that of 1918, and for good reason—I think of the innocent victims of Hiroshima, and of Elizabeth Barrett Browning who wrote:

> Do you hear the children weeping, O my brothers,
>   Ere the sorrow comes with years?

This sorrow is not done.

The war is not over, this is only the beginning of another war, and it is *not* wonderful.